Photo by Neil Benson

Stephen Mailer and Thomas G. Waites in a scene from the
Philadelphia Festival Theatre for New Plays production of
"Minor Demons." Set design by Eric Schaeffer.

# MINOR DEMONS

## BY BRUCE GRAHAM

★

★

DRAMATISTS
PLAY SERVICE
INC.

### SPECIAL NOTE

2

*For Perchalski and Simpers*

*Michael gave me the story;*
*Mark gave me most of the good lines*

*And thanks to Jim Christy, Richard Harden,*
*Andrew Traister and Richard Wolcott for their help*
*in the development of* Minor Demons.

MINOR DEMONS received its world premiere at the Philadelphia Festival for New Plays Theater (Dr. Carol Rocamora, Artistic Director and Producing Director), in Philadelphia, Pennsylvania, on May 3, 1991. It was directed by James Christy; the set design was by Eric Schaeffer; the costume design was by Vickie Esposito; the lighting dsign was by Curt Senie; the sound design was by Jeff Chestek and the stage manager was Scott Lesher. The cast was as follows:

KENNY SIMMONDS ..............................................Stephen Mailer
VINCE DELGATTO ....................................................Larry Joshua
CARMELLA DELGATTO ..............................Karen MacDonald
O'BRIEN ..................................................................Allen Fitzpatrick
MRS. SIMMONDS ..............................................Theresa Donahue
MR. SIMMONDS ....................................................Daniel Richards
DEKE WINTERS ..............................................Thomas G. Waites
DIANE SIKORSKI ..........................................................Mia Dillon

MINOR DEMONS was produced at the Long Wharf Theatre (Arvin Brown, Artistic Director), in New Haven, Connecticutt, on February 14, 1992. It was directed by Richard Harden; the set design was by Hugh Landwehr; the costume design was by Jean Routt and Melinda Watt; the lighting design was by Steven Rust; the sound design was by Brent Paul Evans and the production stage manager was Beverly J. Andreozzi. The cast was as follows:

DEKE ..................................................................Barry Mulholland
VINCE ......................................................................Larry Joshua
DIANE ..............................................................Lauren Thompson
CARMELLA ....................................................Karen MacDonald
KENNY............................................................Nicholas Tamarkin
MR. SIMMONDS ..............................................John C. Vennema
MRS. SIMMONDS ....................................................Callan White
O'BRIEN ................................................................Kevin Cooney

4

MINOR DEMONS was produced at the Arizona Theatre Company (David Ira Goldstein, Artistic Director; Robert Alpaugh, Managing Director), in Tucson, Arizona, on March 23, 1992. It was directed by Andrew Traister; the set design was by Greg Lucas; the costume design was by Francis Kenny; the lighting design was by Rick Paulsen; the sound design was by Brian Jerome Peterson and the stage manager was Elizabeth Lohr. The cast was as follows:

DEKE WINTERS .......................................................Jack Wetherall
DIANE SIKORSKI ...............................................Kathy Fitzgerald
VINCE DELGATTO ...............................John Dennis Johnston
CARMELLA DELGATTO ...................................Evangelia Costa
MR. O'BRIEN.......................................................Dean Thompson
MRS. SIMMONDS ...............................................Diane Kobayashi
MR. SIMMONDS ......................................................Apollo Dukakis
KENNY SIMMONDS ...............................................Aron Eisenberg

# CAST

Kenny Simmonds
Deke Winters
Vince DelGatto
Diane Sikorski
O'Brien
Carmella DelGatto
Mrs. Simmonds
Mr. Simmonds

# SETTING

Time: Winter
Scene: A small town outside of Pittsburgh.

*Minor Dreams* is basically written in the form of a dream. Perhaps nightmare is a better word. Therefore, settings should be suggested and characters can move in and out in a way that suggests a dream state.

# MINOR DEMONS

## ACT ONE

*THE SCENE: A town, somewhere in western Pennsylvania, not far from Pittsburgh.*

*The action of the play shifts constantly. Therefore, simplicity is the best course. Perhaps various geometric shapes to suggest furniture ... I don't know, I'm no designer. Therefore, if the author mentions couch, he is talking about a "suggested" couch. Hand props can be used.*

*Dark.*

*We hear the sound of a train approaching and voices repeating Deke's name: "Mr. Winters ... Mr. Winters ..." The noise grows louder as the lights rise on Deke Winters, who is stretched out on a couch. He appears to be asleep, but restless. He clutches a notebook identical to the one that will be held by Kenny. A cup and saucer are on the floor next to him. The train sound reaches a crescendo.*

DEKE.  *(In his sleep.)* Please! *(He bolts up, letting out a loud gasp. Silence. He is out of breath and sweating. He is fully clothed. The notebook falls to the floor as he reaches for the cup and saucer and takes a drink. Diane enters from behind him, dressed in a bathrobe. She does not say anything.)* I'm okay ...
DIANE.  Come to bed ...
DEKE.  *(A little louder.)* I'm okay. *(She moves towards him. Picks up a cigarette butt from the edge of the couch. He takes another sip from the teacup. Diane watches, not happy.)*
DIANE.  Hungry? *(He shakes his head.)* I can make you some

7

eggs.

DEKE. *(Irritable.)* I'm not hungry. *(She watches as he lights a cigarette.)*

DIANE. It's gonna take time Deke. *(He does not respond. Inhales deeply.)* Give it a week or two, then talk to his parents. They'll know where he is —

DEKE. *(Not letting her finish.)* They don't wanta talk to me Diane.

DIANE. You don't know —

DEKE. If you were them would you wanta talk to me? Huh? Would ya?

DIANE. I'm too tired for cross examination. *(She picks the notebook off the floor.)* This isn't helping you any. Why do you keep looking at it? *(Deke avoids looking at her.)* You wanta do somethin' to help yourself? Rip this stupid thing up and throw it away.

DEKE. Just leave it. *(She tosses it back on to the floor and sits next to him.)*

DIANE. I don't want it in the house.

DEKE. That's ridiculous —

DIANE. Take it to your apartment, take it to the office, I don't care. *(She removes a tissue from her robe pocket and wipes the sweat from his forehead.)* I don't want it in my house. *(He lies down with his head in her lap.)*

DEKE. Okay. *(He lies there for a moment. She runs her fingers through his hair and begins to scratch his head with her fingernails.)* Harder. *(She does.)* If only somebody could invent a valve that you put in the back of your neck ... like in a pressure cooker ... it could let all the steam out of your head when you got tense ... pssssss ... like a balloon. That'd be great. Everything'd be nice and dull ... no more fights ... no more divorce ... no more murder ...

DIANE. No more lawyers.

DEKE. *(Laughing.)* We'd be out of a job, wouldn't we? Oh well ... *(He visibly begins to relax.)*

DIANE. The worst is over Deke. It's just gonna take time. *(He rolls over, turning in to her. Very slowly and very gently, she begins to cradle his head. Lights begin to fade.)* You did the right thing Deke. It doesn't look that way now, it probably never will ... but you did the right thing ... you did the right thing ... *(The voices are heard. Deke, in his still fitful sleep, hears them. At first, the voices are unintelligible, more of an ominous buzz than specific words. Eventually, they become clearer and louder.)*

VINCE.   How could you do this? How?

CARMELLA.   I'm so scared ...

MR. O'BRIEN.   Have any kids of your own Mr. Winters?

MRS. SIMMONDS.   That's no way for any young lady to die ...

MR. SIMMONDS.   That boy didn't kill anybody!

MRS. SIMMONDS.   That's no way for any young lady to die ...

MR. O'BRIEN.   Have any kids of your own Mr. Winters?

VINCE.   How could you do this? How?

CARMELLA.   I'm so scared ...

MR. O'BRIEN.   Have any kids of your own Mr. Winters?

VINCE.   How could you do this? How? *(The voices increase and begin to overlap. The voices rise. Kenny enters and crosses to the notebook. The voices subside. Deke turns to Kenny.)*

KENNY.   You know like how sometimes you just do something really stupid ... you know, really stupid, and you know it's stupid but you do it anyway. You know what I mean, don't you Mr. Winters? That's why I'm giving you this book. It's not that good or anything, just some stuff I wrote. I know you won't show it to anybody — confidential, right? — like you said that day in my room. Anyway ... I want you to have it. *(The lights fade on Kenny. In the dark, we hear the voice of Carmella DelGatto.)*

CARMELLA.   Deke! *(Lights rise on Carmella. She is in her mid thirties, getting heavy and very much a mom.)* Ohhh ... it's good to see you! *(Deke enters the area. He is 38, but looks a little older. His suit, which was expensive and perfectly tailored at one time, now appears a little worn and seems to hang on him. Carmella runs to him, giving him warm hug.)*

DEKE.   How ya doin' Carmella?

CARMELLA.   I'm good — how're you? *(She observes him.)*

DEKE.   Where's your husband?

CARMELLA. He's sittin' out on 208. I just called him on the radio when I heard ya pull up.

DEKE. Runnin' a speed trap?

CARMELLA. *(Shaking head.)* Waitin' for you. *(She points.)* No wonder ya got past 'em — that your car? *(Deke nods.)* What happened to the Mercedes? *(Deke shrugs.)*

DEKE. How're the kids?

CARMELLA. The girls are great. Vincent's a pain in the rear.

DEKE. He's fourteen. That's a requirement.

CARMELLA. They caught him in school the other day with a *Playboy.*

DEKE. Just like his old man.

CARMELLA. Tell me about it. How's Heather? *(A beat.)*

DEKE. Okay. *(She expects more. None comes.)*

CARMELLA. Hope ya don't mind sharin' a room with Vincent.

DEKE. The office got me an apartment out at Silver Lake Terrace.

CARMELLA. That place is filthy. I'll bring the girls out later — we'll give it a goin' over. *(Deke looks out toward his car.)* He oughta be home any minute.

DEKE. Sorry I messed up his surprise.

CARMELLA. Yeah, he was gonna throw the siren on and pull ya over, then come walkin' up and hand ya a six pack. *(Deke laughs.)* You want some coffee?

DEKE. No thanks Carmella. I'm just checkin' in and sayin' hello. I've got a meeting.

CARMELLA. Look ... I better warn ya now, he's gonna give ya some grief about that postcard ya sent — *(From off-stage we hear Vince.)*

VINCE. Welcome home you bastard! *(Vince DelGatto, 38, and dressed in the uniform of a police chief rushes to Deke, picking him up in a bear hug. Vince is a powerful looking man even with the beginnings of a gut around the middle. He wears his uniform casually.)*

DEKE. You wops are too emotional ...

VINCE. Damn it's good to see you! *(He puts him down. Looks at him.)* Jeeezz ... you look like shit. *(Carmella swats him on the arm.)*

CARMELLA.  Vince ...

VINCE.  Well he does. Don't ya think?

CARMELLA.  Yeah, but you're not s'posed ta say it.

VINCE.  Wait'll my mom sees ya. She'll be shovin' pasta down your throat with both hands.

DEKE.  *(Referring to Vince's gut.)* She been doing that to you?

VINCE.  I'm just tryin' to keep up with Carmella. *(A swat.)* Whyn't ya give 'em some coffee?

CARMELLA.  He didn't want any.

VINCE.  How 'bout a beer? I hadda six pack in the car there for ya.

CARMELLA.  Look, you two have fun. *(She kisses Deke, holding his face a moment.)* He's right. You look awful. We'll fatten ya up. *(She gives him another kiss and exits.)*

VINCE.  No wonder ya got by me. That what you're drivin'? *(Deke nods.)* She musta cleaned ya out huh?

DEKE.  I didn't fight it.

VINCE.  Yeah, I was waitin' for ya out on 208 there. You haven't been around for a while. Whatta ya think huh? This town finally gotta mall.

DEKE.  Yeah, I noticed.

VINCE.  Course everybody's outta work. I don't know who the hell's gonna buy anything. *(Throwing his arm around Deke.)* Thinkin' about you the other night. Guess where I busted some kids?

DEKE.  Our spot?

VINCE.  Our spot.

DEKE.  Playin' chicken?

VINCE.  Nahh ... they don't have the guts.

DEKE.  Maybe they're smarter'n we were.

VINCE.  They were puttin' beer bottles on the trestle for the train ta run over. Wimps. Hey, you're comin' over for dinner tonight.

DEKE.  Of course.

VINCE.  Then we'll go over to my parents. They wanta see ya. Who'd you hook up with again? Mom was askin'.

11

DEKE. Ben Gold.

VINCE. That's it. I told her it was one of those Jewish guys. They find a place for ya?

DEKE. Silver Lake Terrace.

VINCE. Place's a pit.

DEKE. *(Nodding.)* I'm still looking for the terrace, let alone the silver lake.

VINCE. I get called out there three, four times a month. Usually some asshole beatin' his wife.

DEKE. Well, I'm one less you'll have to worry about.

VINCE. You're official now huh.

DEKE. She's almost remarried.

VINCE. How 'bout Heather? She in first grade now huh? *(Deke is hesitant.)* You gotta picture of 'er. C'mon, let's see?

DEKE. No ... no pictures. I don't ... have any visitation or anything. *(Vince gives a slightly disapproving look. Deke senses it immediately.)* C'mon. Don't gimmie the dirtbag look.

VINCE. Hey, my cousin Marie just got divorced. You 'member her. Big family scandal right? Del Gatto's don't get divorced; they just put up with each other. She's probably the smartest one inna family. Whatta ya say, I'll give 'er a call ...

DEKE. Hey Vince, I just moved back. Gimmie a couple weeks before ya get me married again. *(A beat.)*

VINCE. So ... where the hell ya been for three months?

DEKE. Around.

VINCE. Don't gimmie "around." That card you sent scared the hell outta us.

DEKE. That wasn't the purpose.

VINCE. We still got it on the refrigerator ...

DEKE. I gotta go Vince. I got a meeting ...

VINCE. "Going away for a while. Call you when I get back." *(Deke starts to move away.)*

DEKE. I'm late ...

VINCE. What the hell was I s'posed to make outta that? Where were ya? *(Deke says nothing.)*

DEKE. What time's dinner?

VINCE. Five-thirty.

DEKE. What can I bring?

VINCE.    Nothin'. I even gotta bottle of Tanquery. We're gettin' loaded. *(Deke laughs.)*
DEKE.    You ready for this? I quit drinkin'.
VINCE.    Yeah. And I turned Irish. *(Deke says nothing.)* Hey ... you're serious, aren't ya? *(Deke nods.)* You really quit? For good? Everything? *(Deke nods.)* No wonder ya look shitty. *(Deke laughs.)* So ... what should I get? Pepsi or somethin'?
DEKE.    Tonic water with a slice of lime. That way I pretend. Gotta go. I have to meet with a Diane Sikorski.
VINCE.    Ohhh ... good luck man. She's a prick.
DEKE.    How can a woman be a prick?
VINCE.    She manages. Five-thirty. *(Deke begins to move away. Lights fade on Vince; rise on office area. Diane Sikorski is behind a desk. She has a folder in front of her to which she refers. She is in her early thirties.)*
DIANE.    Well ... D.K. Winters ...
VINCE.    Hey! Good to have ya back man. *(Vince fades.)*
DIANE.    You look a lot taller on television.
DEKE.    Everybody does.
DIANE.    I'm afraid you're not going to get much media coverage here.
DEKE.    I'm not looking for media coverage.
DIANE.    Really? What are you looking for?
DEKE.    *(Wishing to avoid this.)* Nothing special.
DIANE.    I mean, the usual trend is to move out of a town like this. We don't get many big time Philadelphia lawyers working here. I'm curious.
DEKE.    I grew up here. Look is Ben gonna be in today, I could talk to him.
DIANE.    Ben is never here. I pretty much run the office since he discovered Florida. But he filled me in. You grew up on Connor Street; graduated University of Pitt and you're best friends with our illustrious police chief. *(She tosses the folder on the desk.)* I'm sure he told you a few things about me. We're not exactly the best of friends. He thinks I'm a dyke.
DEKE.    That's between you guys.
DIANE.    He's a lawyer's best friend in this town. His incompetence makes our job a breeze.

DEKE. Think anything you want about my friend Vince, but I'd rather not hear it. *(A beat.)*
DIANE. Do you remember a guy named Laird Duncan? You went to school with him.
DEKE. Yeah.
DIANE. I'm his cousin. When I was a senior in high school he brought me out to Pitt to look around. And he said I had to meet you ... you were the big star of the law school.
DEKE. Did I offer you any sage advice?
DIANE. You looked down my blouse all night and tried to pick me up. You were drunk. Boy, were you drunk.
DEKE. Kind of holding onto a grudge, don'tcha think.
DIANE. Actually, I was very flattered. But then again, I was sixteen. I've been with Ben five years now. It's taken me all that time to be accepted as a competent attorney in this town. Women aren't supposed to be lawyers around here; if you carry a briefcase you're a dyke, ask your buddy. And now that I've built up a reputation, you come along. And I'll be honest, I can't compete with D.K. Winters. I've never represented mob figures, I've never tried a case through the newspapers or on the court steps for the six o'clock news. I know why Ben hired you — you're a real coup for the firm here — but to tell you the truth, I don't expect you to last very long. It's pretty dull around here.
DEKE. We better get some things out in the open here Diane. I don't want your job. I don't want to run the firm. I'm here because I need a paycheck. I'll do wills, divorces, real estate, criminal ... anything that gets thrown on my desk. I won't call any press conferences. I just want to sit at my desk and do my job. I do get a desk don't I?
DIANE. *(Pointing.)* That office over there. You'll have to share a secretary.
DEKE. Fine. *(He rises. She consults folder.)*
DIANE. Daniel Kenneth. Do you prefer Dan or Daniel?
DEKE. My friends call me Deke. It's up to you.
DIANE. Your secretary's Eileen. She'll show you around. *(Deke starts to leave. Stops.)*
DEKE. By the way, if it makes you feel any better Vince

doesn't think you're a dyke. He thinks you're a prick. *(Lights rise on Vince and Carmella at the kitchen table.)*
VINCE.    What'd I tell ya? A regular ball buster. *(She hits him on the arm.)*
CARMELLA.    You wonder why Vincent's got a mouth like he does.
VINCE.    They can't hear me.
CARMELLA.    *(To Deke.)* More coffee?
DEKE.    No thanks.
VINCE.    *(Motioning off-stage.)* Do somethin' with them, will ya? T.V.'s drivin' me nuts.
CARMELLA.    *(Calling off.)* Hey! Turn that T.V. down! *(To Deke and Vince.)* More cake?
VINCE.    You talk to Ben. He'll straighten her ass out.
CARMELLA.    You're worth more there than she is.
VINCE.    Hey! You hear what your mother said? Turn that thing down.
DEKE.    It'll blow over.
VINCE.    I have to come in there I'm gonna smack some butt ... *(To Deke.)* Jesus ... don't ever have kids ... *(He catches himself, glancing at Deke, who simply turns away. Carmella gives him a look.)*
DEKE.    Anyway, it's not worth making a big thing over. She's a little paranoid; I can't say I blame her.
VINCE.    You're gettin' old man. Couple years ago you'dve kicked her ass round the block. *(A hit on the arm.)*
CARMELLA.    Vince ...
VINCE.    I saw his first court case ya know. He was sixteen and he fought a parking ticket.
DEKE.    Not this story again ...
VINCE.    Shoulda seen 'em Carmella. Wearin' a suit up there pointin' out all the things the cop did wrong on the ticket. And he got off too. He always got off. *(Deke is a little uncomfortable.)* You got away with everything.
DEKE.    Come on Vince ... you're borin' the hell outta your wife.
VINCE.    He usta write all my notes for me when we'd skip school.

15

DEKE. *(To Carmella.)* I love being reminded of how I started out as a liar and a forger.

VINCE. Yeah ... I always knew you'd become a lawyer. The best one was the time we stole cigarettes from my old man ... what were we, twelve? And we took 'em out back in the woods. He pulls out a cigarette holder. *(Shaking head.)* You were a weird fuckin' kid ...

CARMELLA. *(The hit.)* Vince.

VINCE. Whatta ya hittin' me ... go hit your kids ... listen to that ... *(He rises.)* I warned youn's ... I'm comin' in there and smack some butt! *(He exits.)*

DEKE. He cracks me up ... playin' dad.

CARMELLA. Yeah. If he smacked butt as much as he says he's gonna he'd a been locked up for child abuse long time ago. *(A beat. She takes his hand.)* He's so glad you're back. He's been like a little kid ever since ya called. *(Deke smiles.)* He went lookin' for ya, ya know. After we got your card. He took a long weekend and drove ta Philly. That's why he was so nuts; your house was sold, nobody at the office knew where ya were ... anyway, he didn't find ya. *(Lowering voice.)* He's not the world's greatest detective. *(Deke says nothing.)* Anyway ... we're glad you're back.

DEKE. Me too.

CARMELLA. But he's right about one thing ... you gotta watch out for that Sikorski woman. She can be real brutal; he knows, believe me. *(Lights begin to fade on the kitchen, rise on Kenny, who is writing in his notebook. Deke observes from the shadows.)*

DEKE. Give it a little time Carmella. I'm just gonna ignore her ...

KENNY. I tried to ignore them ... *(Lights fade on kitchen. Rise on Mr. Simmonds in a different area. He is in his late forties, dressed in work clothes. Although he is in a different area, he talks directly to Kenny.)* I didn't do anything ... I didn't say anything ...

MR. SIMMONDS. What the hell is your problem boy!

KENNY. I didn't do anything! I did what mom said ...

MR. SIMMONDS. Ruth ... what'd you say to him? *(Mrs.*

16

*Simmonds comes in behind her husband. Pale, thin, the same age as Mr. Simmonds.)*

MRS. SIMMONDS.    I told him to ignore them. They'd stop.

MR. SIMMONDS.    They been doin' this for years! Jesus ... I get called at work ... I come to school ... they threw his clothes in the shower ... he's standin' there in the locker room in his underpants cryin' ... why'd ya let 'em do that?

KENNY.    I didn't ... they just took 'em ...

MR. SIMMONDS.    What'd you do? Just stand there cryin' like a little girl. That's what you are pal — a little girl. Gonna start makin' you wear a dress!

MRS. SIMMONDS.    What happened Kenny? *(Mr. Simmonds turns on her. She back away.)*

MR. SIMMONDS.    I just told ya what happened! Why didn't ya fight back?

KENNY.    There was a buncha them ...

MR. SIMMONDS.    So what! How many times I gotta tell ya — kick one of 'em in the balls ...

MRS. SIMMONDS.    Frank ...

MR. SIMMONDS.    SHUT UP RUTH! Just ... shut up ... *(To Kenny.)* I been puttin' up with this shit for years now and I'm gettin' sick of it. You're gonna start fightin' back boy, you understand? You pick up whatever's handy — you understand — you pick up anything and you hit 'em ... *(He mimes grabbing Kenny. Kenny, in his area, reacts, holding up his hands and covering his face.)* You understand boy? *(He slaps. Kenny reacts.)*

MRS. SIMMONDS.    Frank!

MR. SIMMONDS.    Get outta here Ruth! *(She backs away, into the dark.)* You're gonna hit 'em back boy! I don't care what happens — you start fightin' back! *(The lights begin to fade, rise on Deke at his desk with papers.)*

KENNY.    I'm sorry dad ... I'm sorry ... dad ... I'm sorry ... *(Lights fade on Kenny. Diane enters Deke's area.)*

DIANE.    I'm sorry, am I interrupting anything?

DEKE.    Come on in. *(She sniffs.)*

DIANE.    Oh, that's right. Mrs. Stein was here.

DEKE.    She does load up on the perfume, doesn't she?

DIANE.    *(Nodding. She sits.)* Just got off the phone with Ben.

17

DEKE. How is Ben?

DIANE. Tan. He's staying in Florida for Christmas.

DEKE. Does that surprise you?

DIANE. No. But I hope he drops in before Valentine's Day. He's given me the Watson case.

DEKE. Congratulations. *(She says nothing.)* That was an appropriate thing to say, wasn't it?

DIANE. You're a terrific actor. *(He says nothing.)* You knew, didn't you.

DEKE. Yeah, I knew.

DIANE. He offered it to you first, didn't he?

DEKE. *(Nodding.)* Last night.

DIANE. Well, at least you're honest.

DEKE. Somethin' new. Thought I'd give it a try.

DIANE. Why don't you call him back and tell him you'll take it.

DEKE. I don't want it.

DIANE. I thought you needed the money.

DEKE. You've got the seniority around here. It should be your case, it was wrong of Ben to offer it to me. I don't want it. Okay?

DIANE. *(Surveying him.)* Okay. *(She starts to leave, stops.)* I've got a confession to make. I purposely set you up with Mrs. Stein.

DEKE. I figured that. Interesting woman.

DIANE. Pain in the ass, but she's a friend of Ben's so ... anyway, I usually get stuck with her, none too successfully.

DEKE. 0 for four, according to the file.

DIANE. *(Not really pleased that he knows.)* Yeah ... well she comes up with the most ridiculous suits and she never accepts settlement so she always gets beaten in court. I gave her to you so I could watch you lose, and you turn around and talk her into settling. How'd you do it?

DEKE. Professional secret.

DIANE. Come on ... how? *(He motions her to come closer, as if to tell her a secret.)*

DEKE. Charm. *(She lets herself give a small smile.)*

DIANE. I should try it sometime.

DEKE. *(Not looking at her.)* Yeah, you should. *(A beat.)*
DIANE. Plans for the holidays? *(He shakes his head.)* Get to
see your daughter? *(He turns, sharply. Lights rise on Kenny.)*
DEKE. No. *(Diane begins to move away, realizing she has said
the wrong thing.)*
DIANE. Well, have a nice holiday.
KENNY. This year I asked a girl to go to the holiday dance.
DEKE. Yeah, you too — *(Lights fade on Deke. Christmas music is heard. It becomes louder as Kenny speaks.)*
KENNY. Her name is Karen and she's in the ninth grade
and she sits in front of me in study hall on Mondays. She always wears these jeans and these tight shirts that don't come
down all the way so I can see part of her back and sometimes
I see the top of her underwear. She has a little line of hair
that runs down her back and its real light and you can't always see it. So I called her up 'cause I didn't want to ask her
in school. I was pretty nervous. Then her sister answered the
phone. She's in 11th grade and she's real pretty and she
asked who was calling. Then I told her. Then she said hold
on, she said she'd see if Karen was there. Then I heard her
talking to someone, it sounded like Karen. Then she came
back on and said Karen wasn't there. Then she asked me
what I wanted. And I hung up. And the next day at school
she saw me and her and some of her friends started laughing
and then they ran into the girl's room and they laughed. *(The
music grows louder.)* I'm just glad it's Christmas. I really like
Christmas. *(The music stops suddenly. Lights rise on Vince with a
mop in his hand. We are in his basement. He is mopping angrily.)*
VINCE. You kids get to bed or I'm tellin' Santa Claus to
come up there and smack some butt! *(Deke enters.)*
DEKE. Ho, ho, ho ...
VINCE. Lookit this! Whole damn basement's flooded! It's
s'posed to snow on Christmas Eve not rain.
DEKE. Gimmie a broom. *(Vince hands him one. During the
course of this scene they sweep the water.)*
VINCE. We gotta go to her mother's house ... and it's
gettin' late and the kids are gettin' rammy and we all wanta
come home, right? But no, she's gotta sit and talk to her sis-

19

ter ... *(Aimed up the stairs at Carmella.)* Who she talks to twice a day! And I gotta come home and see the basement looks like Johnstown! Aim toward the drain, will ya? *(Carmella enters carrying two beers.)*

CARMELLA.    They're all in bed. You gonna quit yellin'? *(She hands them each a beer. Vince opens his immediately; Deke simply holds his, a bit awkward.)*

VINCE.    We coulda left an hour ago. I still got three bikes and a magic kingdom to put together.

CARMELLA.    You weren't in any hurry to leave your parents.

VINCE.    My mother can cook.

DEKE.    *(Singing.)* Have yourself, a merry little Christmas ... *(They stop. Carmella laughs.)*

CARMELLA.    It's okay Deke. We fight every holiday.

VINCE.    *(Fondly.)* And most of the ones in between too. *(They realize Deke has not opened his beer. To Carmella.)* Whatta ya doin'?

CARMELLA.    I'm sorry, I forgot. Sorry Deke ...

DEKE.    It's okay.

VINCE.    That's real smart Carmella ...

CARMELLA.    I forgot, okay? What can I get ya?

DEKE.    Tonic water ... tea ... anything.

VINCE.    Yeah, get me a pop too. *(He starts to hand her his beer.)*

DEKE.    Don't do that.

VINCE.    I wanta pop.

DEKE.    No ya don't. Drink the beer; I like the smell. *(Carmella starts to exit.)*

CARMELLA.    Mel called. He wants you to call him back as soon as ya can.

VINCE.    Tell 'em I'm cleanin' the pool.

CARMELLA.    He said the O'Brien's called again. She's still not back.

VINCE.    I'll call 'em later. *(Carmella exits.)*

DEKE.    Business?

VINCE.    Girl missin'. Went out to the store, didn't come back yet. She's thirteen. Probably stopped at a party, got loaded on egg nog. I gotta buck says she's in someone's bathroom pukin' her guts up right now. One of the O'Brien kids. Old man's got the insurance place ... you must know him.

DEKE. Oh yeah. *(Vince takes a long swig.)*

VINCE. You sure this is okay? I feel funny doin' this in fronta you.

DEKE. World can't stop drinkin' just because I did.

VINCE. I think about quittin' everytime I getta rotten hangover. Is it tough?

DEKE. Yeah.

VINCE. That what you were doin' for three months? *(Deke says nothing.)* Look I haven't bugged ya 'bout it since the day ya got back. You don't wanta talk about it, okay. Just tell me ta shutup. *(Deke sweeps for moment.)*

DEKE. I was in a hospital.

VINCE. That's what Carmella figured. I was hopin' you were in Tahiti or somethin' but she nailed it. Were you dryin' out?

DEKE. Among other things. C'mere ... *(Vince does. Deke tilts his head back and refers to his nose.)* Look up there.

VINCE. What for?

DEKE. Just do it.

VINCE. Get outta here.

DEKE. Go ahead.

VINCE. Don't go shootin' any boogers at me ... *(He looks.)* What'm I s'posed ta see?

DEKE. Ninety-thousand dollars. *(A beat.)*

VINCE. You're serious?

DEKE. *(Nodding.)* Forty-five a nostril.

VINCE. Jesus Christ Deke ... *(He throws down his mop.)* I mean, I knew you were foolin' around with that shit last time you were back here but ... Jesus ... why didn't ya tell me?

DEKE. What could ya do?

VINCE. I coulda kicked the shit outta ya for starters.

DEKE. I beat ya to it.

VINCE. *(Incredulous.)* Ninety thousand ...

DEKE. Approximately. Dealers don't give receipts. Come on, it's your basement. I'm doin' all the work. *(He hands Vince his mop.)*

VINCE. How the hell could you be so stupid?

DEKE. Easy — it makes ya feel great. That initial rush that ... that fake sense energy ... that's why cocaine is the drug of choice with overachievers. *(He takes out a cigarette.)* And it went with the territory. With the sixteen-hundred-dollar suits and the Mercedes for a second car. And my clients were always more than glad to help me find some.

VINCE. Ahh man I gotta tell ya, that usta piss me off Deke. Seein' ya on T.V. there swearin' all those Mafia assholes were innocent. You knew they weren't innocent. How could ya do that?

DEKE. Part of the job.

VINCE. Don't gimmie that ...

DEKE. Vince, people have no idea what a lawyer's job really is. We're legal hit men, that's all. We're hired to do other people's dirty work. You wanta get even with somebody, hire a lawyer. And they want us to be mean man. They want us to be vicious.

VINCE. And the more vicious ya are the higher the bill, right?

DEKE. Right. And depending upon the client, certain perks. Bags of coke, cases of booze ... thousand dollar a night hookers.

VINCE. You're kiddin'. *(Deke shakes his head.)* What do they do for a thousand bucks a night?

DEKE. Everything.

VINCE. You still with Joyce when all this was goin' on? *(Deke moves away, sweeping.)*

DEKE. My mother — to her dying day — could not make me feel as guilty about things as you could. *(He lowers his voice.)* You mean to tell me you never cheated?

VINCE. I never did, no. And I had opportunities too. *(He takes a swig.)* Listen to me. Opportunities. Four in fifteen years. And two of them were hoggers. *(Another swig.)* I never cheated on Carmella. And that's sayin' a lot comin' from a guy who gets it maybe two, three times a month.

DEKE. *(Smiling.)* You used to get it two, three times comin' home from the movies. You got more action in my backseat'n I did.

VINCE.   Lemmie tell ya, it's easier gettin' it in a backseat than it is with four kids runnin' around. *(They laugh. Vince thinks a moment.)* A thousand bucks? Really? *(Deke nods. Vince shakes his head smiling.)*
DEKE.   What?
VINCE.   Nothin'.
DEKE.   Don't gimmie "nothin'".
VINCE.   Just ... you've done all this stuff. You been places — where the hell've I ever been?
DEKE.   *(Uncomfortable.)* I'm back here aren't I?
VINCE.   Maybe I shoulda gone ta college or somethin', I don't know. I just feel like I never did anything.
DEKE.   You got four nice kids and a wife who puts up with your shit.
VINCE.   *(Smiling.)* Yeah ... yeah. They're good kids Deke. They're a pain in the ass, but they're good kids and I love 'em. But ... I gotta tell ya ... I wouldn't mind spendin' one night with a thousand dollar hooker. *(They laugh.)* Night, hell. Twenty minutes'd be plenty. *(Laughter, then quiet.)* So ... you okay now? You normal?
DEKE.   Not somethin' you ever cure ya just have to ... control it. That's the tough part — facing the fact that part of your brain knows you're doing something incredibly fuckin' stupid and the other part says who cares — chop out another line. Facing the fact that you're out of control ... that's the real bitch. *(A shrug.)* And I've got a few clients in Philly who want my head. I screwed up ... wasn't prepared ... wasn't vicious enough, I don't know. Came very close to getting censured. So I ran away. Typical. Checked myself in, checked myself out. And I came back here ... figured this would be the safest place to come ...
CARMELLA'S VOICE.   Vince! *(She enters, carrying a soda.)* Mel called again ... They talked to the guy at the store. She never showed up there. *(To Deke.)* Diet 7-UP. Okay? *(He nods.)* Somebody saw her talkin' to a kid around 9th and Connor, where they're buildin' the new houses. Mel's got his description.
VINCE.   Tell him to send a car over there to check out all those buildings.

CARMELLA. Since when am I the chief?

VINCE. Okay, you gotta choice. You either make a nice dry phone call, or come down here and play Moses. *(Carmella exits.)*

DEKE. Look if you gotta go, I'll do this ...

VINCE. Nahh ... nothin' serious. Christ, it's Christmas Eve, the kid's just loaded some place. I gotta admit, I been lucky. Only one really crazy case since I took over. Couple months ago this kid — seventeen — rapes a 74-year-old woman then slaps her around with a ball peen hammer for kicks. Know what he got? Huh? Know what he got? Six months in juvie 'cause he's four months shy of 18. That fair?

DEKE. I didn't hear the case Vince ...

VINCE. The little bastard was guilty Deke. Trust me on this, all right. He was guilty. That old lady's in a home now ... she's scared ta death of everything ... barely gets around on a walker. Six months, that fair Deke?

DEKE. Let's not get into this again ...

VINCE. Guess who his lawyer was? Your bitch boss. Put that old lady on the stand with that shithead who raped her sittin' fifteen feet away and badgered the hell outta her. Got her all confused, turned things around makin' it out to be her fault. She shouldn'ta opened the door ... she shouldn'ta let 'em in ... why did she have a ball peen hammer in the living room? Shit like that.

DEKE. That's her job man —

VINCE. Bullshit. Lemmie tell ya, I got her in the hallway afterwards — made sure there's no witnesses — and I told her I hoped to have the pleasure of comin' to her house someday and findin' her like I did that old lady.

DEKE. That was smart.

VINCE. You didn't see what she did to that woman. I'm tellin' ya Deke, you're my best friend and I love ya ... but you're a lawyer and you're scum.

DEKE. That does it. I'm returning your present.

VINCE. You guys have totally screwed up the whole country. Lawyers — take 'em out and shoot 'em. *(Carmella enters.)*

CARMELLA. Vince, the O'Brien's are down at the station.

They wanta talk to ya ...

VINCE. There's nothin' I can do Carmella. Let Mel handle it.

CARMELLA. You're the chief — they wanta talk to you. They're worried.

VINCE. It's Christmas Eve ...

CARMELLA. Vince, it's their daughter. *(A beat.)*

VINCE. Tell 'em I'll be there as soon as I get some dry shoes on. *(She exits.)*

DEKE. Don't worry. I can put a bike together.

VINCE. Hope they're not nuts. People expect miracles, ya know. God forbid you even suggest the kid might run away. You be here when I get back?

DEKE. Probably. *(He starts to leave, stops.)*

VINCE. Okay if I tell Carmella about ... where ya were? I mean, she kinda knows ...

DEKE. Sure.

VINCE. Look, you ever get like that ... or like, ya know ... you get a craving or something — you call me. I don't give a shit what time it is. I know I'm not a doctor ... I'll just ... I don't know, handcuff ya to the water heater or somethin'. Okay?

DEKE. Okay. Go to work.

VINCE. I sure hope this kid's passed out at some party ... *(Lights fade, rise on Kenny.)*

KENNY. I did this one real stupid thing.

VINCE. *(As he leaves.)* Merry fuckin' Christmas huh?

KENNY. There was this aquarium in science class with all these fish in it and I sat in the back right near it and one day I just turned up the temperature thing a little. And the next day I turned it up a little more and it stayed that way all weekend and when we came back on Monday all the fish had died. It was like they'd been boiled. I didn't think it would kill 'em or anything I just wanted to ... see what would happen, that's all. Then Mr. Korzek got real mad and tried to find out who did it. I think he suspected everybody but me. That's pretty funny huh? Ha-ha ... *(Lights down on Kenny. A flash bulb goes off and Vince is seen in full uniform. More flashes*

*go off as the lights rise.)*
VINCE.    Okay. I have a short statement to make. I can't take
any questions. "At 12:30 p.m. today, December 26, the body
of Christine O'Brien was found in a construction site on the
corner of Ninth and Connor. Preliminary coroner's report
states the girl had been dead approximately 48 hours. Mul-
tiple blunt injuries of the head, neck and trunk were the
cause of death." That's all for now. *(Begins to exit, stops.)* Yes
... we do have a suspect in custody at this time ... *(Waving for
quiet.)* That's all I can say right now! *(More flashes.)* I'm sorry,
I can't answer any questions! *(Lights rise on Deke. Vince crosses
towards him.)*
DEKE.    Will somebody give me a straight answer?
VINCE.    What'sa problem counselor?
DEKE.    Two bozos at the front desk who don't want to let
me in.
VINCE.    They got orders Deke. Place is crawlin' with report-
ers. We gotta nasty little murder here if you haven't heard.
DEKE.    I heard.
VINCE.    And we nailed the guy too, but he's underage so
we gotta be careful 'bout releasin' his name. Heaven forbid
the little son of a bitch should get some bad p.r.
DEKE.    Where is he? *(Vince stares at him.)*
VINCE.    Ahh no.
DEKE.    Where is he Vince?
VINCE.    My office. Parents are with 'em.
DEKE.    Thanks. *(He begins to move away.)*
VINCE.    Hey, give up on this one Deke. Let someone else
have it. You don't need this aggravation.
DEKE.    I'll talk to you later Vince.
VINCE.    Let's put it this way. We've got the weapon, the fin-
gerprints, the confession ... *(Lights rise on Kenny and Mrs.
Simmonds in the office.)*
MRS. SIMMONDS.    What did you tell them Kenny? *(Kenny
says nothing.)*
VINCE.    And the family ain't rich. *(Lights fade on Vince.)*
MRS. SIMMONDS.    Chief DelGatto says you told him you
did it. Is that true Kenny? *(Nothing.)* Is that true? *(Deke enters,*

*carrying briefcase and folder.*)
DEKE.   Mrs. Simmonds, I'm D.K. Winters.
MRS. SIMMONDS.   (*Slightly flustered.*) Yes ... yes, hello. I know
who you are ... I knew your mother when she worked at the
library. (*Deke is engrossed in the file.*) She was always very
nice ...
DEKE.   (*Looking up.*) Thank you. Hello Ken, I'm Mr. Winters.
I'm going to be representing you.
MRS. SIMMONDS.   Say hello Kenny. We call him Kenny.
Can't you say hello to Mr. Winters?
KENNY.   (*Very quietly.*) Hi.
DEKE.   Hi. (*To Mrs. Simmonds.*) Where's your husband?
MRS. SIMMONDS.   He went to get me something to eat.
I'm sorry — he'll be back in a minute. I'm a diabetic and I
have to ... I'm sorry.
DEKE.   That's all right.
MRS. SIMMONDS.   He shouldn't be long ...
DEKE.   It's okay. (*He moves to Kenny.*) Kenny, do you mind
talking to me for a few minutes?
KENNY.   Okay. (*Deke makes notes.*)
DEKE.   First of all, do you understand what you're being
charged with?
KENNY.   Uh-huh.
MRS. SIMMONDS.   The chief says he confessed but he won't
tell me anything ...
DEKE.   Mrs. Simmonds, we're getting ahead of ourselves
here. One step at a time, okay?
MRS. SIMMONDS.   I'm sorry.
DEKE.   Now I know a lot has happened to you in the last
few hours, but try and remember as best you can. Do you
know the name of the officer who arrested you?
KENNY.   It was the chief and another man. He was younger.
I don't know his name.
DEKE.   Did the chief inform you of your rights? Do you
know what I mean by that?
KENNY.   Like on Miami Vice?
DEKE.   Right ... like on Miami Vice. Did he read them off
a card?

27

KENNY. Yes.

DEKE. Did you understand them?

KENNY. *(Nodding.)* Sure. We did that stuff in school. Bill of Rights.

DEKE. Did he at any time deny you access to a phone? *(Kenny is not sure.)* Did he let you make a phone call?

KENNY. Yes.

MRS. SIMMONDS. He called us. *(Deke turns to her.)* I'm sorry.

DEKE. Did the chief, or any other officer make any kind of threats. Did they push you around at all ... did they frighten you? *(Kenny shakes head.)*

KENNY. They weren't mean or anything.

DEKE. Did they allow you to use the bathroom when you had to?

KENNY. I didn't have to.

MRS. SIMMONDS. He'll go all day without using the boy's room at school. He waits until he gets home. I don't know how he does it.

DEKE. Listen Kenny, I'm going to have to ask you to do me a big favor ... *(Vince and Mr. Simmonds, carrying a sandwich and some candy bars, enter.)*

VINCE. Mr. Winters you only have a few minutes. We have to get the young man to juvenile by five o'clock. *(He exits.)*

MR. SIMMONDS. I'm Frank Simmonds. I spoke to you on the phone.

DEKE. Yes, how do you do.

MR. SIMMONDS. Got you some Milky Ways Kenny. *(Kenny takes them. Says nothing.)* They're your favorites, aren't they?

DEKE. Mr. Simmonds, I only have a few minutes. *(He turns to Kenny.)* I want you to do me a favor, okay Kenny? I don't want you to talk to anybody without me being there. That goes for anybody, understand? That goes for policemen or doctors or other lawyers. You just very politely say that you can't talk to anyone without me being there.

MRS. SIMMONDS. Frank ...

MR. SIMMONDS. Ruth, the man's talking.

MRS. SIMMONDS. My sandwich. I need my sandwich. I'm

sorry ... *(He hands it to her.)*

DEKE.   That even goes for the other kids at juvenile hall.

MR. SIMMONDS.   They're not going to send him there. You know what those other kids'll do to him in a place like that? *(Deke lights a cigarette.)*

DEKE.   I'm working on it Mr. Simmonds. *(Vince re-enters.)*

VINCE.   We have to go Kenny.

MR. SIMMONDS.   Our lawyer just got here.

VINCE.   He can talk to him at juvenile hall Mr. Simmonds. Come on Kenny. *(Simmonds steps between Kenny and Vince.)*

MR. SIMMONDS.   You're makin' a big mistake here DelGatto. *(Vince speaks to Deke, calmly.)*

VINCE.   Counselor, you might want to warn Mr. Simmonds here that unless he gets out of my way he can be charged with obstructing an officer. *(Simmonds and Vince stare at each other.)*

DEKE.   Mr. Simmonds ... *(Simmonds moves out of the way.)*

MR. SIMMONDS.   *(A mumble.)* Big mistake ...

VINCE.   Let's go Kenny.

KENNY.   You know, you really smoke too much Mr. Winters. We saw a movie about it in school.

MRS. SIMMONDS.   Kenny!

DEKE.   It's okay Mrs. Simmonds. You're right Kenny. *(Kenny crosses to Vince. Mrs. Simmonds hugs him. Kenny is embarrassed.)*

KENNY.   I'll be okay mom.

DEKE.   *(To Kenny.)* Don't forget what I told you.

KENNY.   I won't.

VINCE.   Put your arms around your back Kenny. *(Kenny obliges. Vince pulls out handcuffs. Mrs. Simmonds reacts, Deke shoots Vince a look. Vince ignores him.)*

MR. SIMMONDS.   You don't have to do that!

VINCE.   Standard procedure Mr. Simmonds.

MR. SIMMONDS.   That boy can't hurt anybody! *(Vince escorts him out.)* Can he do that?

DEKE.   I'm afraid so.

MR. SIMMONDS.   That dago sonovabitch ... I don't know who the hell was dumb enough to make him chief ...

DEKE.   *(Sharply.)* Mr. Simmonds you keep your opinions

about Chief DelGatto to yourself. Do we understand each other? *(Simmonds backs away.)*

MR. SIMMONDS. *(A mumble.)* That boy didn't kill anybody ...

DEKE. Now, bail is not going to be easy with a charge such as this, but it's not impossible. Do you own a home?

MR. SIMMONDS. Yeah, I own a home.

DEKE. Would you be willing to put it up?

MR. SIMMONDS. Course I would. That kid's not goin' anywhere.

DEKE. Okay. Now, this will not stay out of the papers for long. Knowing this town, it's already common knowledge. You're going to start getting some harassment.

MRS. SIMMONDS. Why?

MR. SIMMONDS. Ruth!

DEKE. *(Gently.)* Because that's the way people are Mrs. Simmonds. When you get strange phone calls, you just hang up. Don't say anything. Same goes for reporters — not a word. They keep bothering you, call me.

MR. SIMMONDS. I'll tell them my son didn't do it!

DEKE. Not a word. You're his father Mr. Simmonds, and no one is going to believe a word you say, so say nothing! Understand?

MRS. SIMMONDS. We understand.

DEKE. What do you do for a living Mr. Simmonds?

MR. SIMMONDS. Maintenance. Down the mill.

DEKE. Can you get some time off?

MR. SIMMONDS. We're on shutdown this week. Maintenance has to be there.

DEKE. See what you can do. It'd be better if you just stayed at home this week. Now, I've got some work to do before everything closes for the day. Any questions before I go?

MR. SIMMONDS. No.

DEKE. Then I'll call you the minute I know something.

MRS. SIMMONDS. Mr. Winters ... *(She is unsure.)*

MR. SIMMONDS. Ruth, the man's in a hurry.

MRS. SIMMONDS. *(With great difficulty.)* I heard ... I heard out there ... they said that that girl ...

MR. SIMMONDS.   Don't take all day Ruth.

DEKE.   It's all right Mrs. Simmonds. Go ahead.

MRS. SIMMONDS.   They said that she had been ... molested. *(Almost a whisper.)* Sexually molested.

MR. SIMMONDS.   That's ridiculous.

MRS. SIMMONDS.   Is it true? I'd rather hear it from you than read it in the paper.

DEKE.   There is ... some preliminary appearance of molestation. It'll take another day or so for the autopsy to be completed. We won't know for sure until then.

MRS. SIMMONDS.   I see. Thank you. *(Deke moves away from them.)*

MR. SIMMONDS.   If I honestly thought he'd done ... this ... this thing ... then he shouldn't be allowed back out on the street — I believe that. But my boy couldn't do something like that Mr. Winters. *(Lights begin to fade on the station area.)* A person lives under your roof all his life don't you think you get to know whether or not he's capable of such a thing. *(Lights out on the office area. Light remains on Deke. Lights rise on Diane in bathrobe with towel around her head.)*

DIANE.   Can't this wait?

DEKE.   No. This Simmonds case — why me?

DIANE.   Hey, you're the big name —

DEKE.   *(Sharp, controlling.)* I got a great idea: I go down the hardware store, buy a vice, bring it back here and let you put my balls in it. Then maybe we can talk to each other like adults for a change. *(Silence.)*

DIANE.   The father asked for you.

DEKE.   This case has got six o'clock news written all over it.

DIANE.   You should be used to that.

DEKE.   I don't want that anymore. I told you that when I first got here.

DIANE.   I figured you just said that to appease me.

DEKE.   I'm serious Diane, I really don't think I want this case.

DIANE.   You said you'd do anything I threw on your desk.

DEKE.   You can't trust me I'm a lawyer. Why don't I get him out on bail and you take over, okay?

DIANE.   No.

DEKE.   Come on, you'll love the publicity.

DIANE.   I'm not that experienced at criminal. Especially homicide.

DEKE.   You had some.

DIANE.   Right. And they were bad experiences.

DEKE.   The ball peen hammer case?

DIANE.   So, you talked to your friend, huh? *(Deke says nothing.)* I really should become a prosecutor. I'm finally beginning to realize that I don't enjoy defending guilty clients.

DEKE.   Wait for innocent ones and you'll starve.

DIANE.   I did a number on that poor woman ... I really did. Everything they drill into us about rattling a witness even if you know she's telling the truth. From what I hear that was one of your specialties.

DEKE.   "Methods of Cross Examination." Solid A.

DIANE.   Low B. *(She shrugs.)* Well, everything I did to that woman was perfectly acceptable — legally. "Problems in Legal Ethics." Solid A.

DEKE.   I went to school before Watergate. The course wasn't offered. *(She laughs. He smiles.)* You did what you were supposed to. If you're gonna let something like that bother you ...

DIANE.   I'm not like you — I don't get off on makin' people squirm —

DEKE.   You been judgin' me since the day I got back here. What is your fuckin' problem —

DIANE.   *(Blurting.)* You make me nervous! Okay? You do. I can't ... pinpoint what it is but ... God, you bother me sometimes. I'm not even sure you're aware you do it ... but ... you do. *(A beat. Deke shrugs.)*

DEKE.   Old habit. *(Silence.)*

DIANE.   You've got the experience all over me on this one. You'll give him the best defense.

DEKE.   Somebody else then ...

DIANE.   You've done tons of this stuff. What's the matter? *(He tosses the folder on the table.)*

DEKE.   This. *(She picks it up.)*

DIANE.   Pretty brutal?

DEKE.   Nothing out of the ordinary. Buried her alive after sexually abusing her with what appears to have been a jagged lead pipe. Your typical Christmas Eve in a small town.

DIANE.   My God ...

DEKE.   And that's not even the sick part. It's the kid. Kenny Simmonds looks like he stepped off a box of Corn Flakes. I've represented a lot of killers Diane. Guys who did it for a living and showed absolutely no remorse ... no conscience, they'd all go out to dinner after a big hit. But you looked at them and you talked to them ... and you knew they were killers. You knew they were capable of it. This kid ... I mean, you look at him and ya wish he lived next door so he could babysit for ya. I met him for five minutes and I just ... I don't know ...

DIANE.   Look, if you're really serious I can put someone else on it. But I honestly think you're the best person for it. I really do Deke. *(Deke says nothing.)* Can I get you a drink or something?

DEKE.   No thanks.

DIANE.   So ... what's the verdict? *(Deke says nothing, picks up the file.)* Thank you.

DEKE.   Look, I shouldn'tve bothered you at home, I'm sorry. You're probably goin' out.

DIANE.   Not for a while.

DEKE.   It's just that I can't talk to Vince about this ... *(He smiles.)* I don't know what made me think I could talk to you about it.

DIANE.   I think we just had a very civil ... minute and a half. That's a record for us.

DEKE.   Yeah ... *(He gets up to leave.)* Big date?

DIANE.   My father. We go bowling every Thursday. He doesn't drive too well at night anymore so ... you know, I go into Pittsburgh and pick him up. Do you bowl?

DEKE.   Everybody raised in this town bowls.

DIANE.   Would you like to come with us. *(Deke says nothing.)* Maybe if I saw you in bowling shoes you wouldn't make me nervous.

DEKE.    I've got work. And I'm defrosting a Swanson Hungry Man dinner. Kind of the highlight of my week. *(Begins to move away.)* Talk to you later.

DIANE.    Hey look ... uhh, I'm throwing a little party for New Years ... nothin' big, couple people from the office, some neighbors. Stop in if you want.

DEKE.    Well ... thanks. We'll see. *(He moves away as the lights fade on her.)*

DIANE.    And ... ya know, feel free to bring a date if you want. *(Lights begin to fade. Nicholas O'Brien, late thirties, well dressed ... a small town success story. He steps out of the darkness suddenly, startling Deke.)*

O'BRIEN.    Mr. Winters. I'd like to ask you a few questions if you don't mind.

DEKE.    I'm afraid I do. I've already made a statement, that's all I can say for now.

O'BRIEN.    I'm not a reporter. I'm Nicholas O'Brien.

DEKE.    Of course ... I'm sorry Mr. O'Brien, I didn't recognize you.

O'BRIEN.    That boy. He's out on bail?

DEKE.    Yes.

O'BRIEN.    Why?

DEKE.    Mr. O'Brien, I'm very sorry for what happened to your daughter. I'm not even going to say I understand what you're going through because I don't ...

O'BRIEN.    That boy is at home now. I know the house, I drove past it today.

DEKE.    Please, for your own peace of mind, I'd suggest you stay away from ...

O'BRIEN.    It looks nice and warm. The house. *(Deke stares at him, unsure.)*

DEKE.    I can't discuss the case with you at this time. I'm sorry. *(A beat.)*

O'BRIEN.    They've predicted snow for tonight. *(Deke says nothing. Attempts to move away.)* Going down to 12 degrees, according to the radio.

DEKE.    Yes ...

O'BRIEN.    My wife picked out a very pretty, pale yellow

dress for Chrissy. Summer dress, light. I thought she should be in something warmer, but my wife ... is very fragile at the moment — which I'm sure you can understand — and I thought it best not to argue with her. Must be awfully cold in a metal box ... in the ground. Wouldn't you agree?

DEKE.    I have to go Mr. O'Brien. I'm sorry ... I have to go.

VINCE.    *(To the television.)* Come on! Hit somebody for Chrisesake!

O'BRIEN.    Have any kids of your own Mr. Winters?

DEKE.    No. *(Lights fade. Lights rise on Carmella and Vince on their couch. Deke just sort of wanders into the picture. There are empty beer cans around. Vince appears a little drunk. The are watching television.)*

VINCE.    Come on! Check that sonuvabitch! *(Reflex. Carmella's smack on the arm.)*

CARMELLA.    You don't even like hockey. You just watch it for the fights. You decide about New Year's?

DEKE.    I don't think I'm gonna make it.

VINCE.    Aww come on Deke. Don't stick me with her relatives by myself.

CARMELLA.    You goin' somewhere?

DEKE.    *(Uneasy.)* Nothing special.

VINCE.    I invited my Cousin Marie for ya ... come on, she's divorced. They all put out.

CARMELLA.    Quit buggin' him.

VINCE.    I'm not buggin' him. Am I buggin' ya?

DEKE.    Yeah.

CARMELLA.    See? *(She rises.)* Anybody hungry?

VINCE.    That's her way of sayin' she's hungry. She figures if she gets it for us it don't put any weight on her.

CARMELLA.    *(Ignoring him.)* Deke, you hungry?

DEKE.    Hell yes. We haven't eaten anything in at least a half hour. *(She exits.)*

VINCE.    Hey, bring in that pepperoni my old man gave us, willya hon? *(To Deke.)* Wait'll ya taste this thing. Clean your system right out. *(Silence for a moment.)* So, you still pissed or what?

DEKE.    What about?

VINCE.    I saw ya yesterday. When I put the cuffs on that little bastard. Ya shot me the dirtbag look.

DEKE.    You coulda waited 'til you stepped outta the room.

VINCE.    What for? Why should I?

DEKE.    How'd you like to see your son in cuffs?

VINCE.    I'm never gonna see that.

DEKE.    You don't know that. We did a little breakin' the law when we were kids, remember? We just didn't get caught.

VINCE.    We didn't murder anybody.

DEKE.    Just think of the mother next time ...

VINCE.    I'll think about Mrs. O'Brien, okay? You worry about the Simmonds broad. *(At the T.V.)* Come on! Hit 'em back! *(A beat.)* You'll be gettin' a new autopsy report tomorrow.

DEKE.    I really don't wanta talk about it, okay Vince?

VINCE.    Change in the time of death.

DEKE.    What? What change?

VINCE.    Oh ... now you wanta talk about it huh? Well, don't go gettin' a hard on ... it's not gonna help your client. Time of the attack is still the same. They put death at somewhere Christmas morning. Five thirty, six o'clock ... just about when we were finishin' up the last bike ... *(Deke says nothing. Carmella enters, unnoticed, carrying a tray and beer.)* I went over there that night ... I went over and I looked around that building myself. I was in there. And she was still alive. I just waved my flashlight around, ya know ... I didn't see anything. She was there all right ... still breathin' ...

CARMELLA.    You're not on duty. Knock it off, okay?

DEKE.    Yeah, listen to her for a change. *(She hands him the beer.)*

CARMELLA.    Here. *(She sits. There is an awkward silence, the only sound comes from the T.V. Deke moves away.)*

VINCE.    Oh, by the way ... the chain keeps fallin' off Vincent's bike. I'm thinkin'a gettin' a lawyer and suin' your skinny ass. *(Lights begin to fade. Lights rise on Kenny in his room. He is writing in a green notebook. Deke crosses to Kenny's room.)*

MRS. SIMMONDS.    Kenny! Kenny, Mr. Winters is here. I'm sorry the house looks like this Mr. Winters ... but I've just

been awfully tired ... *(Silence.)* Kenny, can't you say hello?
KENNY.   Hi.
DEKE.   Hi. This has got to be the neatest teenage boy's room I've ever seen.
MRS. SIMMONDS.   Kenny does it all by himself, don't you Kenny? All I do is change the sheets. He does all the rest himself. Will this room be all right for you to talk? You can have the living room if you want ...
DEKE.   This is fine. I thought it would be better here than the office.
MRS. SIMMONDS.   Well ... I'll leave you to your business then. Kenny, you answer all Mr. Winters' questions, okay?
KENNY.   Okay.
MRS. SIMMONDS.   I'll uhh ... I'll be downstairs then I guess. *(She exits. During the first few minutes of this scene, Deke closely observes the room. Kenny does not move.)*
DEKE.   Does it bother you when people call you Kenny?
KENNY.   No.
DEKE.   That's my middle name — Kenneth. First is Dan. I used to hate it when people called me Danny.
KENNY.   Doesn't bother me.
DEKE.   What're you writing?
KENNY.   Story sort of. Diary stuff.
DEKE.   You like to write?
KENNY.   It's okay.
DEKE.   How did it go at the Juvenile Hall?
KENNY.   Okay. Nobody bothered me or anything. *(Deke puts an unlit cigarette in his mouth.)*
DEKE.   Did you talk to anybody?
KENNY.   You told me not to. You can light it if you want. It's okay.
DEKE.   I think I'll just hold it awhile. You were right; I ought to cut down. *(Deke surveys the room.)* Steelers fan huh?
KENNY.   *(A shrug.)* Dad buys me that stuff. He bought me the T.V. too. Yesterday. So I can watch it up here. *(Deke takes a small tape recorder from his briefcase.)*
DEKE.   Okay. What we're going to do now is sort of an interview. I'm going to tape it. Is that okay with you?

KENNY. Sure.

DEKE. *(Turning it on.)* Now, what I want you to do is tell me everything you told the police the day you were arrested.

KENNY. *(A shrug.)* I just did it. That's all. *(There is not a shred of emotion in his voice. Deke pauses.)*

DEKE. Yes, I know Kenny, but I have to have your story in your words. And try and tell me exactly what it is you told the police. Don't change anything for me. Try and put it in as close to the same words as you told them, okay?

KENNY. Okay.

DEKE. And I'll be throwing in some questions.

KENNY. Okay.

DEKE. Now ... it's Christmas Eve day. Let's start in the afternoon. Say around four o'clock. What were you doing?

KENNY. I was down the basement. I stole some of dad's beer.

DEKE. Why? *(Kenny does not answer.)* To give it to Chrissy? *(Kenny nods.)* So you went out intentionally looking for her.

KENNY. *(Matter of factly.)* Oh yeah. She goes down the store to buy the paper every afternoon.

DEKE. You've been watching her? *(Kenny nods.)* How long?

KENNY. While.

DEKE. Did you think she was pretty?

KENNY. Yeah.

DEKE. Why did you steal the beer?

KENNY. Just to drink it. *(Deke looks at him a moment; Kenny looks directly back at him. Deke leans over and turns off tape recorder.)*

DEKE. I can't help you if you're gonna lie to me.

KENNY. I'm not lyin' —

DEKE. Yes you are —

KENNY. No I'm not — honest. *(Deke simply stares at him. Kenny smiles.)* How'd ya know?

DEKE. I just did.

KENNY. No, come on —

DEKE. *(A little louder.)* I just did.

KENNY. 'Cause I never get caught when I lie. Like at

school, if I didn't finish my homework or somethin' — everybody believes me.

DEKE.  Well, I used to be sort of a pro when it came to lying Kenny, so don't pull any fast ones, okay?

KENNY.  *(Sizing him up.)* Okay.

DEKE.  Maybe I should explain something to you; everything you say to me is confidential. Just between you and me. Absolutely confidential — that's protected by law.

KENNY.  I don't have to talk to you though, do I? If I don't want to. And they can't make me say anything at a trial, can they? *(Deke observes him a moment.)*

DEKE.  So ... where'd you get your law degree?

KENNY.  *(Smiling.)* T.V.

DEKE.  Well, you're right. You don't have to talk to anybody — not even me. *(He stands, picking up his briefcase.)*

KENNY.  Mr. Winters ... if I tell you things ... you promise not to laugh or anything?

DEKE.  I won't laugh.

KENNY.  Okay. *(Deke sits back down, picking up the tape recorder.)*

DEKE.  We don't have to use this if it makes you uncomfortable.

KENNY.  I don't mind. Confidential, right?

DEKE.  Right. *(He turns it back on, refers to legal pad.)* Why did you steal the beer?

KENNY.  'Cause ... she'll do it to you if you give her beer.

DEKE.  You mean sex?

KENNY.  Yeah. She'll do sex with you if you give her beer. That's what I heard. Kevin hadda party around Thanksgiving and they went into the bathroom and ... she did it.

DEKE.  And you wanted to have sex with her?

KENNY.  *(Nodding.)* Don't tell my mom or anything, okay Mr. Winters. Please.

DEKE.  It's all right Kenny. Keep going. *(The lights dim on Deke. He is always seen in a muted light. The lights change on Kenny. He rises and begins to act out the rest of the scene.)*

KENNY.  Well ... I saw her on the way to the store. "Hi

Chrissy. Merry Christmas ... " and she says somethin' like "Hi Kenny ... " and keeps moving. She won't stop to talk to me. *(His actions now start matching his words.)* So I show her the beer I had in my school bag. "Let's go in the houses here and drink." *(Chrissy's voice — which is strangely accurate.)* "I have to get the paper for my father." "Come on ... just one beer. I want to talk to you about somethin.'" "What about?" "Not here. Come on. It's dry in here ... " So she follows me.

DEKE.   Where exactly did you go?

KENNY.   The basement part. It's not all finished, and one wall is only half up, but it's pretty dry. "Where'd ya get the beer?" "I bought it." I wanted her to think ... you know, that I could get beer. So I give her one and I have one, but I don't drink it. I hate the taste, I just kinda sip it. "So what'd you wanta talk to me about?" So ... well, I don't know how to start. So I tell her I heard about Kevin's party. "What'd you hear?" And I told her. "Yeah, well nothin' happened. That's all a lot of bullshit." She said that Mr. Winters, not me. And then ... *(his voice trails off.)*

DEKE.   What Kenny?

KENNY.   I just decided to do it. *(Deke lights a cigarette.)* "Get your fucking hands off me!" I pushed her and she tries to get past me and I push her and I keep pushing her 'til we're up against the wall and I pushed her again and I ripped part of her shirt open ... *(A scream.)* "Leave me alone! Please ... " And I can see she's really scared of me. She is, she's really scared of me ... so I kept pushing her 'cause she wouldn't shutup 'til finally she stopped. I put her on the ground next to the wall that wasn't all built, there was some rain coming in. So I undid her pants ... you can't say anything about this Mr. Winters ... and I try to pull them down. And I can't get them down ... they're too tight. So I keep pulling and her back is getting all muddy 'cause the rain's coming in harder.... And I yank and yank and I can't get 'em down, so I just sort of ... rip them. By the zipper there. And they open up far enough to ... see it.

DEKE.   Go on Kenny.

KENNY. But I'm still not sure what you're s'posed to do so I remember this book I saw once where there was this lady and she was usin' this thing ... so I picked up this piece of pipe ... you know, just so I could get started.... She started to scream. So I got on top of her to stop it ... and I'm pushing ... and she's so scared of me! ... but I can't stop her screaming so I reached up and got hold of part of the wall and it's lose. I can feel it, and I pull back, and part of it comes down. There were bricks. And she stopped screaming, so I kept pulling down the bricks and the rain started coming in and there was a big pile of bricks on the ground so I figured I'd better get out of there because it was a big hole and I'd get in trouble if anybody knew I did it. So I left. *(Silence. Deke stubs out cigarette.)*

DEKE. Where did you go?

KENNY. Home. I had to get changed. We went to my grandmother's for dinner.

DEKE. Is this all you told the police? *(Kenny nods.)* Okay, day after Christmas. Tell me what happened.

KENNY. Well ... I saw all the police cars over by the houses, so I went over.

DEKE. Why did you do that?

KENNY. To see what was going on.

DEKE. But you knew. Didn't you think that was dangerous?

KENNY. Didn't really think about it.

DEKE. Okay. Keep going.

KENNY. There were a few people standing up against this yellow ribbon thing so I got up to the front there when Chief Del Gatto came out of the building and told us to move back. And when I did he looked down and asked me what kind of sneakers I was wearing. So I told him Converse. And he asked me if a lot of kids wore them and I said yeah and he said 'cause there were footprints in the building there that looked just like them and I said they were probably mine because I had been in there the other night when it was muddy. And he asked me if I was in there alone and I told him Chrissy was with me. So he asked me if I'd get in the police car with him a minute to talk.

DEKE.  Why did you tell him about the footprints?

KENNY.  I don't know. I just sort of ... it came out like I wanted to tell him or something. Honest.

DEKE.  What happened after you got in the car?

KENNY.  That's when I told him what I told you. And he let me go into the building and I showed him the pipe. Then we went down to the station and he got me a pop and then he came back in with some other man and read to me from that card and I called my parents.

DEKE.  Do you mean your rights? He read them to you from the card?

KENNY.  Right.

DEKE.  So he didn't read them from the card originally, he just said them.

KENNY.  No.

DEKE.  What do you mean?

KENNY.  I mean he read them to me. That was the only time he did it. *(Deke rises and crosses to him.)*

DEKE.  Kenny, this is very important. Are you sure he read them to you at the police station? *(Kenny nods.)* And you confessed in the police car? And gave him the pipe then.

KENNY.  *(Nodding.)* You know there aren't handles on the inside of a police car. I mean, in the back. They have to get out and open it for you ... *(Lights begin to fade on Kenny as he keeps talking. Deke moves to another area, lighting another cigarette.)* And then my parents came down and mom was crying and then you came and told me not to talk to anyone ... *(His voice and the lights fade. Deke sits at another part of the stage, smoking and staring. Suddenly, the sharp sound of a noisemaker. Deke jumps. Diane enters, carrying a bag and wearing a party hat.)*

DIANE.  Didn't know you were still here. Putting in overtime? *(She models the hat.)* Whatta ya think? Is it me? Every year I put away all the hats and noisemakers someplace special so I can use them the next year and every year I forget where I put them. In some obscure corner of my house there are about three years worth of tacky hats and noisemakers. *(Deke says nothing.)* I'm gonna grab a quick dinner. Want to join me. *(Silence.)*

DEKE.    I can get him off. *(He laughs.)* I can ... I can get him off ... *(Laughs a little louder.)* I can get that crazy little bastard off ... *(Lights fade.)*

**END OF ACT ONE**

# ACT TWO

*Flash bulbs go off illuminating both Deke and Vince at op-
posite ends of the stage. O'Brien is in the middle. Loud
sound of questions being shouted.*

VINCE.    I think it stinks, that's what I think!

DEKE.    I'm sorry, I have nothing to say ...

O'BRIEN.    I'm not qualified to discuss the legal aspects.

VINCE.    This isn't jaywalking ... we're talking sexual assault
and murder. Bail should not be allowed in these cases.

DEKE.    No comment ...

O'BRIEN.    If bail is legally acceptable ... then ... I accept it.

VINCE.    Things in this country are pretty screwed up when
a murderer — ahh, excuse me — alleged murderer can just
walk out of jail.

DEKE.    No comment.

O'BRIEN.    What I can not accept ...

VINCE.    The hearing has been set for January 4th.

O'BRIEN.    Is the added pressure being applied by you
people.

VINCE.    There's really nothing to say until that time.

DEKE.    No comment ...

O'BRIEN.    The constant phone calls —

VINCE.    Well, thank you. To be honest, I was a little surprised at just how fast the whole thing was solved too. *(He
laughs. He is enjoying this.)*

O'BRIEN.    Reporters and ... cameras following our every
move —

VINCE.    Solving any case involves a lot of work and a little
luck.

DEKE.    No comment.

VINCE.    I'm just glad it is solved. This is a nice town here
— we wanta keep it that way ...

DEKE.    No comment! *(Lights fade on Deke and Vince; remain
on O'Brien.)*

O'BRIEN. I think you would all agree that I ... that my family and I ... *(He smiles violently, looking for the right words.)* Are in an ... unpleasant situation — to say the least, am I right?
DEKE. No comment.
O'BRIEN. And seeing my daughter's school picture in your newspapers everyday ... *(He restrains.)* Let's just say it's not helping the wounds heal any faster. Please ... please think of my family and stay away from my home. *(Lights fade on press conference and rise on Kenny and his notebook.)*
KENNY. My dad brought me home this T.V. for my room. That's the weirdest part about this whole thing, the way my dad's been. He started lettin' me bring food up here. I wasn't allowed to do that before. He said we'd get bugs or something. So I stay up here most of the day. They don't think I should go outside yet. But I don't see what the problem is because I went out on the porch the other day to watch the snow and I saw some of the kids from school. They weren't like friends or anything but I knew them so I waved and they just walked away real quick like they were afraid of me or something. And you can see cars slowing down when they pass the house to look. Like I was famous or something. That's pretty funny huh? Ha-ha ... *(Lights fade on Kenny and come up on Vince's house.)*
VINCE. Your mother hadda bring in the trash cans today. That's your job pal, ya unnerstand? Don't let me hear you made mom bring in those trash cans again.
DEKE. Anybody home?
VINCE. Come on in. Just yellin' at my kid. *(Sees Deke looking at newspaper.)* Whatta ya think, huh? Front page. I know it don't compare to somea your clippings, but hey, I'm not greedy. 'Ya wanta know what the best part of this is. *(He waves the paper.)* You missed all the fun around here when they went to make me chief. Lotta people were pissed off ... said they oughta bring in somebody from the outside ... somebody who went to college, right? I just barely got the job and things weren't too smooth the first month. Check this out. *(He turns pages.)* Even an editorial. This paper wasn't too crazy about me neither but lookit this. "Through the alert police work of

45

Chief DelGatto, a suspect was apprehended less than an hour after the crime had even been discovered." *(He laughs, smacking the paper.)* My old man's gotta 'bout thirty copies — all over the kitchen table. *(Deke says nothing.)* You want some coffee or somethin'?

DEKE.     No thanks. I gotta talk to ya Vince ...

VINCE.     Go ahead.

DEKE.     About the case.

VINCE.     Hey, that ethical? We don't wanta do anything unethical.

DEKE.     Kinda private. Is Carmella around?

VINCE.     Gettin' her hair done. New Year's Eve ... I might even get laid tonight. *(Deke does not laugh.)* What'sa problem?

DEKE.     First of all, this conversation never happened. Okay?

VINCE.     Depends. Whatta we talkin' about?

DEKE.     I shouldn't be here, I should just go out and do my job. But before I do I gotta ask you some questions. But it's off the record, okay?

VINCE.     Yeah, okay. What?

DEKE.     We might have a technicality.

VINCE.     Hey, don't gimmie that. Nobody laid a hand on that kid. I hadda witness with me the whole time.

DEKE.     It's not that ...

VINCE.     Don't get me wrong. I would've liked to have strangled the little bastard right there.

DEKE.     Miranda, Vince. We're talking the Miranda here. *(Vince stares at him a moment, then laughs.)*

VINCE.     He got his rights, Deke.

DEKE.     There's the problem. He says you gave him them to him after he confessed.

VINCE.     *(Immediate, urgent.)* Bullshit!

DEKE.     That's what he told me.

VINCE.     Ohh ... that's what he told you, hanh? Well, "he" also shoved a lead pipe up a thirteen year old girl! You think he's gonna be above tellin' a fúckin' fib! What's the matter with you Deke? Jesus ...

DEKE.     Then why would he tell me that?

VINCE.     Stuff like that's on T.V. alla time. Read a newspaper once in a while — people are always gettin' off for stupid things like that. The kid's not dumb ... nutty as a goddamned fruitcake, but he's not dumb.

DEKE.  Okay, you tell me.

VINCE.  Tell ya what?

DEKE.  When did you read him his rights?

VINCE.  What's your problem?

DEKE.  I'm just askin' ya a question.

VINCE.  I don't believe this. I don't believe this — this sick bastard's tryin' ta get off and you're helpin' him any way ya can.

DEKE.  Look, you wanta take a swing at me go ahead, but answer the goddamned question.

VINCE.  Right in fronta the house there! Happy? Soon as he showed me his footprint I read him his precious fuckin' rights.

DEKE.  You're sure?

VINCE.  Everybody there saw me! Call Sam — go ahead, call him! — he was the other arresting officer. He was right there! Go ahead, call him! *(Deke says nothing.)* I realize he's just a cop and you got the word of a fifteen year old kid who pulled a brick wall down on a girl ...

DEKE.  All right ... all right ...

VINCE.  Any idiot knows to read 'em his rights. Whatta ya think — I'm stupid? I know I never went ta college ...

DEKE.  Stop it, okay! I hadda check. I didn't know. I mean ... ya hadda great suspect right there — I figured ya mighta got excited and forgot.

VINCE.  Well I didn't. And I got witnesses.

DEKE.  You're sure?

VINCE.  Fuck off Deke! You're here in my house callin' me a liar!

DEKE.  I'm not callin' ya a liar!

VINCE.  I never lied to you man!

DEKE.  Look, I wouldn't even be here if it was anyone else Vince. I shouldn't even be talking to you about it, but I'd rather clear it up now than at the hearing in front of a buncha newspapers where it'd just embarrass the hell outta you. If you're tellin' me the truth, great. We've got no problem.

VINCE.    Whatta ya mean if?

DEKE.    Okay ... I'm sorry ...

VINCE.    No! Whatta ya mean "if"?

DEKE.    There's no mention of Miranda in your report.

VINCE.    I probably gotta couple spelling mistakes too. I'm not a secretary Deke.

DEKE.    It just doesn't look good.

VINCE.    You think I'm lyin' to you?

DEKE.    I hadda check.

VINCE.    How long you know me? Hanh? I ever lie to you? Huh? I ever lie to you?

DEKE.    No.

VINCE.    Jesus Deke ... you know things about me Carmella don't even know. I couldn't lie to you if I wanted to ... you'd see right through it.

DEKE.    Okay ... forget it. *(More to himself as he moves away.)* Forget it.

VINCE.    Forgotten. *(Lights fade on Vince.)* Hey Deke ... even if I didn't give 'em his rights, what difference would it make? The little bastard's guilty ... *(Diane appears, a coat over her shoulders, drink in her hand. She is a little drunk.)*

DIANE.    I thought you left.

DEKE.    Gettin' a little air. *(She crosses towards him.)*

DIANE.    You're not having a good time, are you? Well, neither am I, tell ya the truth. *(No reaction.)* You're not going to hurt my feelings. I know I throw boring parties ... I've never been much of a hostess. That's why I only get drunk at my own get-togethers. Gives me the illusion of having a good time and I don't have to drive home. *(A beat.)* Aren't you cold?

DEKE.    I'm never cold. Look, I don't mean to ... it's your party, why don't you go back in.

DIANE.    I don't want to go back in. You're the only person I was having fun talking to. *(She drinks.)* You're not drinking are you?

DEKE.    No.

DIANE.    Don't worry about driving. You can always stay here.

DEKE.    I don't drink anymore.

DIANE.    Not at all?

DEKE.    I'm an alcoholic. *(A beat. She moves to put her drink down.)* Don't. Please. *(She picks it back up.)* The word — alcoholic. I mean, I've said it a few times in the privacy of my therapist's office but ... I've never even said it to Vince. He knows but ... just ... the word.

DIANE.    It's nothing to be ashamed of.

DEKE.    Logically, I know it's a disease. Emotionally, I still think it's a weakness and I used to hate weakness. You were right about me; I could smell it in people. I'd get 'em on the stand there and I'd destroy 'em and the whole time — inside — I was snearin' at 'em. I thought I was so much better ... so much smarter. I'd sit right there in my office sippin' vodka from a coffee cup in front of important clients. That's why I always had to have a huge desk — keep people far enough away. And I'd convince myself that because I was drinking from a coffee cup ... I wasn't really drinking. *(He lights a cigarette.)* I don't hate weakness anymore.

DIANE.    May I have one?

DEKE.    You don't smoke.

DIANE.    Only when I'm drunk. Oh ... sorry.

DEKE.    It's okay.

DIANE.    I just feel funny all the sudden. Here you are telling me something very serious and I'm ... loaded. *(She looks at the cigarette.)* No filter?

DEKE.    Sorry. *(He lights it for her.)*

DIANE.    I've spent about six weeks now trying to figure you out.

DEKE.    Save your energy.

DIANE.    I thought you were going to be pushy and obnoxious. And you aren't. I'm disappointed. I worked up a great resentment for nothing.

DEKE.    Should've met me a few years ago.

DIANE.    I did. You were pushy and obnoxious. *(He laughs. She inhales.)* These are pretty rough. *(He moves away from her; she shivers.)*

DEKE.    Go back to your party.

DIANE.   Not yet.

DEKE.   Don't stay out here on account of me. I'll be going in a few minutes.

DIANE.   It's not even midnight. You that bored? *(He shrugs.)* Come on, what is it? You don't like my French onion dip.

DEKE.   I just oughta go. *(He tries to move away. She takes his arm.)*

DIANE.   What's the matter Deke?

DEKE.   Nothing.

DIANE.   You come to my party, you stand outside half the night ... won't even wear a funny hat. *(A beat.)* What's the matter?

DEKE.   You'll be sorry you asked.

DIANE.   Try me.

DEKE.   Kenny Simmonds.

DIANE.   That's what I figured. Did you talk to your friend?

DEKE.   Yes.

DIANE.   That wasn't wise.

DEKE.   And he claims he did Mirandize him.

DIANE.   And?

DEKE.   What?

DIANE.   Any corroboration?

DEKE.   Come on, it's a party. Stop trying to sound like a lawyer. *(She says nothing.)* Talked to the other cop. He backs Vince up.

DIANE.   One cop backing up another cop. There's a surprising chain of events.

DEKE.   You know, it's hard carrying on a serious conversation when the other person is covered with streamers ... *(He removes some from her hair. She playfully pushes his hand away.)*

DIANE.   Come on ... that was all carefully placed to make me look festive. *(She holds onto his hand a moment, looking at it.)* My God ... you gnaw your nails.

DEKE.   *(A shrug, moving away.)* Tryin' to cut down on the smokes.

DIANE.   So ... do their stories check? *(He stares at her a moment.)*

DEKE.   You love this, don't you?

DIANE.   What?

DEKE.   Most of us grow out of the Clarance Darrow phase our first year clerking, but you ... you really love all this moral/ethical/legal crap, don't you.

DIANE.   I never made the big bucks. Let me have some fun. *(Stubs out her cigarette.)* Next time I ask for a smoke, turn me down. *(He smiles. Says nothing.)* Don't screw yourself up here Deke. Do the stories check?

DEKE.   Okay ... okay, what if Vince did forget ... okay? What if? I mean ... it's not like he beat a confession outta the kid ... what if he made a mistake? An honest mistake. Huh? What's right then counselor? Answer me that.

DIANE.   *(Quietly, shaking her head.)* It's a stupid question.

DEKE.   No it's not —

DIANE.   Okay, today we let an honest mistake go by ... next week a dishonest mistake ... *(A beat.)* Did you know that a recent survey shows that lawyers are the most hated profession in the United States? Swear to God, most hated profession, we're number one. Dentist's are number two — we're number one. I have a little trouble dealing with that. *(She looks over at him. He laughs softly.)* What?

DEKE.   Nothing.

DIANE.   You know why people hate us? This is my theory; we complicate things. Without us life would be so simple ... because ... because I don't think most Americans deserve to be Americans — they don't and you know why? This is my theory; democracy makes you think and most Americans don't like that — they don't — they're stupid! They want a king or something to make all their decisions for them so they don't haveta face a Kenny Simmonds gettin' away with it. Off with his head — who needs a trial. Trials make you think ... *(She pauses.)* I have this really shitty attitude, in case you hadn't noticed. I've never really dealt well with people — maybe that's why I throw lousy parties, I don't know. But it really pisses me off that everybody hates us ... *(Patting his leg.)* Bet that little tirade made you feel better, huh?

DEKE.   Not just the case. Everything lousy gets magnified over the holidays. I hate the holidays ... miss my daughter.

DIANE.   You've stopped drinking. Visitation shouldn't be hard to arrange. I'd be glad to handle it —

DEKE.   I can have all the visitation I want. Just don't want it. *(Stubs out his cigarette; lights another.)*

DIANE.   You don't mean that.

DEKE.   Joyce's almost remarried, Heather adores the guy. I just confuse her. She doesn't want anything to do with me.

DIANE.   *(Laughing uncomfortably.)* That's ridiculous.

DEKE.   Quite a normal reaction for a five-year-old who watched daddy smack mommy around. *(He laughs.)* Add cocaine addict to alcoholic. And one morning I came home after being up four days straight — that's the truth Diane, four days — and the only reason I came home at all was because mommy had cancelled all daddy's credit cards. Daddy — it seems — was totally out of control, but it was hard to explain that logically to daddy after he's gone approximately ninety-six hours without sleep. Kicked in the door as they were eating breakfast and ... my wife tried to ... calm me down I guess, but I was in no mood for that and I ... hit her ... I hit her in the face ... and I backed her up against the sink ... I coulda' killed her just then, and she knew it ... and then I looked over at Heather, who was sitting there in her little pajamas just staring at me. She didn't run ... didn't say a word ... didn't cry. Just stared. That was the worst part. I mean ... she shoulda been scared of me — I'd never done anything like that before — never. But she looked at me as if she wasn't even surprised that I'd just hit her mother. No hysterics — calm. Like she expected me to do something like that all along. *(Without it appearing in his voice, he has started to cry. Diane moves closer to him.)* That's when I realized what I'd turned into. And I couldn't blame the booze or the coke — I did then — but it was me. Something ... in me. *(Smiling.)* That little revelation cost me seventeen-thousand dollars in therapy. Therapy ... exorcism might be more appropriate. *(He laughs; she does not.)* So I came back here where it's safe, and everything's goin' pretty good and then ... I meet this kid. *(Urgent.)* This kid ... he's unravelling everything. Vince's the only family I've got and now ... he lied to me. *(His voice trails off.)* God, I wanta drink. *(He moves away from her.)* I used to hate crying drunks and look at me. I don't even have that for an excuse. *(She touches his face. He is embarrassed.)* I better go —

DIANE. *(Looking at watch.)* Not yet. Come on, it's not even midnight ... *(Looking at him.)* You're not gonna believe this. We missed midnight.

DEKE. That figures.

DIANE. New Year's kiss? *(She kisses him gently. He kisses back, she responds. He clutches her.)*

DEKE. I'm sorry ... I'm sorry ... it's your party ...

DIANE. And you can cry if you want to.

DEKE. Thank you for inviting me.

DIANE. Don't leave.

DEKE. I can't go back in there.

DIANE. Neither can I.

DEKE. You sure?

DIANE. No. *(She kisses him.)*

DEKE. What about your guests?

DIANE. They'll lock up. *(Lights fade. Lights rise on Kenny.)*

KENNY. Up to now the only thing that really bothers me is my mom. She seems really nervous when she talks to me. Yesterday I went downstairs when she was ironing and I guess she didn't hear me and I said hi and she jumped and knocked over the ironing board. The whole board. And it's not like she says anything but she stares at me all the time like at dinner. She looks scared or something. *(Lights begins to fade, rise on Carmella.)* That's the only thing that really bothers me.

CARMELLA. Something's bothering him Deke. He's been in a funk since New Years.

DEKE. Kids home?

CARMELLA. Tina's upstairs.

DEKE. Keep her there for a while, okay?

CARMELLA. Why — you guys have a fight or somethin'? *(Deke says nothing.)* Let me tell ya somethin' — it has not exactly been a lot of fun around here the last couple days. He hasn't been sleepin' right, he's been barkin' at the kids, and

... so, you wanta tell me what's goin' on with you two guys? *(Deke moves away — she touches him.)* He tell ya Kenny Simmonds and Tina had a study hall together? Hmm? Mighta been her Deke. I want things back to normal around here ...

VINCE.  Hey ...

CARMELLA.  So you ... you do somethin' about this, okay?

DEKE.  Hey ...

VINCE.  How's your New Years? Get laid or anything?

DEKE.  How was yours?

VINCE.  Same old shit. Midnight, Carmella's uncle comes downstairs dressed likea baby, ya know, banner across 'em. I mean, it was funny the first ten years but get a new bit. *(Deke says nothing.)* You want coffee or somethin'?

DEKE.  No thanks. Had a little talk with Sam.

VINCE.  *(Smiling.)* Right after ya left here. Nice to know I'm trusted.

DEKE.  Don't start.

VINCE.  Ya feel better now? *(Deke says nothing.)* Hanh? Can we go back to bein' normal again? *(Deke takes a deep breath. Vince stares at him, sipping beer.)*

DEKE.  Now I want you to do me a big favor:  don't deny that you lied to me, okay?

VINCE.  Hey, wait a minute —

DEKE.  *(Louder.)* I've had two days to punch walls and I'm fine now ... *(Softening.)* I know how strongly you feel about this ... and I know you're worried about the repercussions ...

VINCE.  That's got nothin' to do with it ...

DEKE.  Just don't deny it! Okay? *(A beat.)*

VINCE.  Right here ... you and me — the truth. Yeah, you're right, okay? I gotta little anxious, I forgot. Shoot me, I made a mistake. I was a little too busy puttin' away a killer to worry about legal crap.

DEKE.  Don't editorialize Vince. We gotta problem.

VINCE.  What's this "we" shit — you're sittin' pretty. I'm the one's gotta watch his step. *(He laughs; Deke does not.)* I shouldn'ta lied to ya. I panicked, okay? For a minute I treated ya like a real lawyer and not ... ya know — you. *(Silence.)*

DEKE.  At the hearing tomorrow I'm gonna have to move

that all evidence be suppressed as tainted because my client was not advised of his rights at the time of questioning. *(Vince looks at him unsure, then smiles.)*
VINCE. Okay ... okay ... ya did your job. *(He puts Deke into an affectionate headlock.)* Ya scared the hell outta me, alright? For a minute there I thought you were serious. *(He begins a little roughhousing. Deke does not play along.)* I learned my lesson, okay? I'll write it onna board a hundred times: "I will give the little scumbag his rights." Okay, hanh? Now let's just forget it.
DEKE. I'm serious.
VINCE. What? *(No answer.)* Come on, don't gimmie "serious." You do somethin' like that, that kid'll get off —
DEKE. I have to —
VINCE. You know what they'll do ta me? Hanh? *(Deke moves away. Vince stares at him, still not comprehending.)* Jesus ... you'll do anything ta win, won't ya?
DEKE. It's not that —
VINCE. Okay, okay. This conversation never took place, right? You said so. So, here with you — the truth. Tomorrow in court, I go back to the other story.
DEKE. You can't do that Vince.
VINCE. Watch me.
DEKE. Your witnesses didn't back you up. You got to Sam, but you didn't get to them.
VINCE. Then don't call any witnesses!
DEKE. I have to —
VINCE. Go ahead then, call 'em. Sam and me'll be enough.
DEKE. I'll rip him apart on the stand Vince! You know I will. I've had 20 year F.B.I. vets up there and I've made them piss themselves *and they were telling the truth!* Whatta you think I'm gonna do to a rookie cop who's lyin'?
VINCE. This town's gonna believe us 'cause they wanta believe us.
DEKE. That's not good enough Vince. I'm talkin' about perjury.
VINCE. People lie alla time in court. You know it!
DEKE. That's not the point.

VINCE. You never hadda client lie?
DEKE. That has nothin' to do —
VINCE. Answer the question! *(Deke rises.)* Where ya goin'?
DEKE. You'll probably be gettin' a call from the D.A. in a little while. You gonna be home?
VINCE. Siddown will ya?
DEKE. He'll be told that the two cops are perjuring themselves and that will be proved on cross examination. He'll also be shown Sam's report, which was rewritten pretty badly. *(A beat.)*
VINCE. *(Stunned.)* Whatta ya sayin'?
DEKE. How ya been sleepin' Vince?
VINCE. You playin' games?
DEKE. You haven't been sleepin' too well I hear. You usta be able to sleep in the middle of Connor Street and now you're havin' trouble. *(Vince stares at him, not believing.)*
VINCE. Why you doin' this to me?
DEKE. I'm not doin' anything to you Vince! I'm tryin' ta keep ya out of jail!
VINCE. Bullshit!
DEKE. Then fuck you Vince ... get up on the stand with your story and see what happens ...
VINCE. Ya smell a big one, huh — get back on T.V., right?
DEKE. Believe anything ya want —
VINCE. Just get offa the case Deke! That's all ya gotta do — I'll take it from there.
DEKE. That won't do it Vince. They'll just get another lawyer. And if the guy's got half a brain he'll ask the same questions and get the same answers and see the same holes in the stories and he'll figure out that it's alla bunch of fucking lies. And you'll get nailed for perjury and — who knows — maybe you won't actually do time, but you'll never work as a cop again. Anywhere. Wanta put your family through that Vince?
VINCE. What is with you? Since when are you Mr. Fucking Honest?
DEKE. I just can't lie anymore! I've spent my whole life lyin' and if dryin' out taught me nothing else it taught me I can't keep lying! 'Cause once I do it starts all over again and

I'm dead.

VINCE.   So ... what'm I s'posed to do?

DEKE.   Tell the truth. Get on the phone to Sam, tell him
to go back to his original story and his original report and I
won't say a thing about any of this....

VINCE.   Mighty white of ya ... *(Vince picks up his beer and
stares at him.)* How 'bout a beer Deke? Hunh ... how 'bout a
beer.

DEKE.   Just tell the truth Vince. That's not askin' a lot ...

VINCE.   That sounds pretty funny coming from you, man.
*(Lights rise on Mrs. Simmonds and begin to fade on Vince.)*

MRS. SIMMONDS.   I don't understand any of this Mr. Winters ...

VINCE.   How you been sleepin', Deke?

MRS. SIMMONDS.   I'm sorry, but I don't understand.

DEKE.   It's not a trial; it's a hearing. I'd rather just go
through this once — where's your husband?

MRS. SIMMONDS.   He'll be down in a minute. What's going to happen Mr. Winters?

DEKE.   It's sort of like a preliminary trial. Testimony and
evidence is presented to see if there's enough to go to trial.

MRS. SIMMONDS.   Is there?

DEKE.   That's what we have to talk about ...

MR. SIMMONDS.   *(Yells from off-stage.)* Get out goddamnit!
GET OFF MY LAWN! *(He enters, angry, still putting on his suit.)*
Goddamn it Ruth, they're all over my lawn! *(He starts to exit.)*

DEKE.   Mr. Simmonds ...

MR. SIMMONDS.   You're a lawyer goddamnit! Get them out
of here ...

DEKE.   Just ignore them ...

MR. SIMMONDS.   It's not your lawn! *(Unnoticed, Kenny enters,
wearing a suit.)*

MRS. SIMMONDS.   We'll go out the back ... *(Mr. Simmonds
ignores her, moving to other side of stage.)* They've been out there
everyday. And when it's not them it's people from the town.
Constantly.

MR. SIMMONDS.   Get off my property damnit! I'll sue your
asses! My boy's innocent! NOW GET OFF MY LAWN!

KENNY. Mom, could you help me with this? *(They both react. They didn't know he was there. He holds out his tie.)*
MRS. SIMMONDS. Oh Kenny ... my hands hurt today. Get your father to help you.
DEKE. C'mere Kenny. I'll help you. *(He moves behind Kenny, reaching over.)* Can only do it from this angle. *(Mr. Simmonds re-enters.)*
MR. SIMMONDS. Moved 'em back to the street.
DEKE. Congratulations Mr. Simmonds. You just made the six o'clock news statewide.
MR. SIMMONDS. You're our lawyer — why can't you do something about them?
DEKE. I've told you what to do Mr. Simmonds — you ignore them. They get bored and they go away. But you don't seem to believe me.
MR. SIMMONDS. *(Moving to Kenny.)* I'll do that. *(He tries to tie Kenny's tie from the front.)*
DEKE. All right, I'd like to explain what is going to happen at the hearing because the press is going to swoop down on us after it's over and I want you to do exactly as I tell you. *(To Mr. Simmonds, who is botching up the tie.)* Understood?
MR. SIMMONDS. It's not your son ...
DEKE. You want to do it? Huh? You've got all the goddamn answers! You go to court! Here! *(He picks up his briefcase, shoving it at him.)*
MR. SIMMONDS. You can't talk to —
DEKE. SHUTUP GODDAMNIT! FOR ONCE JUST KEEP YOUR FUCKING MOUTH SHUT! You haven't done a thing I've asked you to help your son — you've done nothing but make my job harder *and it's hard enough already!* Now we do what I say from here on or you can do it yourself. Understand? *(Silence. Kenny stares at Deke a moment, smiling. Mr. Simmonds gets behind his son and attempts the tie again.)* At the hearing I am going to move that all evidence be excluded as tainted because your son was not informed of his rights.
MRS. SIMMONDS. What evidence is there?
DEKE. *(Ignoring her question.)* What we're doing is perfectly legal. It's not a trick or anything, but it's going to stir up a

lot of people. You've got to be prepared for that.

MRS. SIMMONDS. What does that mean Mr. Winters? I'm sorry ... I just don't ...

DEKE. There won't be a decision today, but it should mean that there will be no trial.

MR. SIMMONDS. That means he's innocent.

DEKE. It means there'll be no trial. *(He crosses to Mr. Simmonds.)* It means not a word. In the courtroom, on the courthouse steps, on the front lawn ... nothing. Nothing. *(A beat.)*

MR. SIMMONDS. I'll bring the car up back.

KENNY. *(Holding untied tie.)* Dad ...

MR. SIMMONDS. Get your mother to do it Kenny. *(As he exits.)* Why can't you wear clip-on ties like everybody else?

MRS. SIMMONDS. *(Looking off.)* I'm sorry.

KENNY. That was really somethin' — you yellin' at dad.

MRS. SIMMONDS. You forget that happened Kenny. Wait in the car. We'll be out in a minute.

KENNY. Okay. *(He smiles at Deke.)* That was really somethin' ... *(He exits.)*

MRS. SIMMONDS. Mr. Winters ... I'm not the brightest person in the world. *(She smiles, nervously.)* And I'm having a lot of trouble understanding this ... not just the legal things ... but ... all of it ... and since it happened ... no one tells me anything ... Frank and I never talk about it ... I don't think I've said three words to Kenny ... you've been very nice, but I still don't know what's going on! *(Directly at him.)* What evidence Mr. Winters? ... what? ... they said something about a confession, and if there was a confession then ... that would mean ... that he ... I'm scared of him Mr. Winters ... I'm in my own house with my son and I'm scared ... I'm sorry I ... did he do it? *(Deke says nothing.)* He did, didn't he? He did that to her ... that ... terrible ... I'm sorry, I don't understand this ...

DEKE. Mrs. Simmonds when this is all over ... *(He gropes, unsure.)* You have to get Kenny some help Mrs. Simmonds. Do you understand what I mean? Psychiatric help —

MRS. SIMMONDS. Frank doesn't believe in that ...

DEKE.     I'm not talking as your lawyer now. I'm talking as
another person. And you have to believe me Mrs. Simmonds,
I know what I'm talking about. *(Deke moves away as lights rise
on Vince.)*
VINCE.     I just have a statement — I can't take any questions.
DEKE.     For God's sake Mrs. Simmonds ... get your son some
help ...
VINCE.     A motion has been made to suppress certain evidence concerned with the Christine O'Brien case because the
suspect was not advised of his Constitutional rights. I take full
responsibility for not immediately reading him his rights. It's
not as if I don't know basic police procedure ... but there was
a lot of confusion at the scene of the crime ... and the procedure was not followed. This was a grave mistake. And I'm
not the first police officer to make it ... but that don't ... uhh,
doesn't make it right ... *(Lights rise on Deke and O'Brien.)*
O'BRIEN.     You're a very smart man, Mr. Winters.
VINCE.     And as chief, I take full responsibility. *(Lights fade
on Vince.)*
DEKE.     I can't talk to you Mr. O'Brien.
O'BRIEN.     Yes you can Mr. Winters. You just don't want to.
*(Deke attempts to pass; O'Brien grabs his arm.)* What're you trying
to pull here?
DEKE.     Don't do that. *(O'Brien lets go.)*
O'BRIEN.     My wife wasn't at the hearing because our other
daughter went back to school today and ... she felt she had
to call there three or four times to make sure she was all
right. *(A smile.)* That's overreacting a bit, wouldn't you agree?
But then again, she does have a lot of time on her hands
since all she does is sit and stare at Chrissy's Christmas pre-
sents. She won't even let me take down the tree ... *(Deke moves
away from him.)*
DEKE.     I can't talk to you ... *(He lies down on the couch.)*
O'BRIEN.     Rest easy Mr. Winters — there's nothing I can do
to you. After all, you're a lawyer, am I right? *(Diane moves to
Deke, rubbing his back.)* But that uneducated ... greasy police
chief of ours ... him I can do something about.

DIANE.    That bad, huh?
O'BRIEN.    And I will Mr. Winters!
DEKE.    Oh yeah. *(Lights out on O'Brien.)*
DIANE.    *(Massaging.)* I can feel it. *(She digs in especially hard. Deke reacts.)* Don't be such a baby.
DEKE.    Is O'Brien shooting his mouth off or can he actually do something?
DIANE.    Not by himself, but he's got friends on council. He was one of them who didn't want Vince in the first place. *(She bends back his shoulder; he reacts.)*
DEKE.    Why don't you just tie me to the back of the car and get this over with.
DIANE.    Stop fighting me. Relax.
DEKE.    What do you think they'll do to him?
DIANE.    God Deke, I don't know. You grew up here. What do you think?
DEKE.    I think they're gonna nail him to a cross.
DIANE.    You don't know for sure. I got a lot of harassment for defending certain people. It dies down.
DEKE.    That's because they can't do anything to you. Vince they can get to. Things are black or white in this town ... no gray areas. Last week Vince was the big hero ... as soon as that decision comes down ... forget it, he's dead around here. People love to nail cops.
DIANE.    There are other places ...
DEKE.    He lives here Diane. His family's here. *(Lights rise on O'Brien, Mr. and Mrs. Simmonds.)*
DIANE.    People have short memories.
DEKE.    Not around here.
O'BRIEN.    To the editor ...
DEKE.    They're gonna nail him ... *(Lights fade on Deke and Diane.)*
O'BRIEN.    Today the court has released a person suspected of murdering my daughter due to lack of evidence. We will never know the truth.
MR. SIMMONDS.    Happy? Of course I'm happy. I've been saying it all along: my boy is innocent!
O'BRIEN.    My family and I are cognizant of the fact that the

highest courts in the land are taking stands to protect the individual ...

MR. SIMMONDS.  You can't live under the same roof with someone and not know whether or not they're capable of something like this ...

O'BRIEN.  Though in our personal grief we do not agree with the law, we realize that the basic concept of our democratic form of government is such that, in protecting all individuals, injustice will occasionally occur within the system when mistakes are made.

MR. SIMMONDS.  We're just glad it's over with.

O'BRIEN.  Therefore, I am requesting your extreme consideration that the individual responsible be removed from office ...

MR. SIMMONDS.  *(To Mrs. Simmonds.)* Aren't we? We just want to get things back to normal.

O'BRIEN.  And that a properly trained person who can enforce the laws and protect our community be appointed in his place.

MR. SIMMONDS.  Of course we're not going to move. Why should we?

O'BRIEN.  For the protection of the people in this town, I request that you take action in this matter.

MRS. SIMMONDS.  *(Quietly.)* I just feel very bad for the parents of that girl.

O'BRIEN.  My family has suffered a loss that we can never overcome.

MRS. SIMMONDS.  That's no way for any young lady to die. *(Lights fade on the Simmondses.)*

O'BRIEN.  In the name of God, do not let a tragedy like this happen again. *(Lights rise on Kenny in his room, writing in his notebook. Deke approaches.)*

DEKE.  Kenny?

KENNY.  *(Reacting.)* Hi Mr. Winters. Kinda surprised me.

DEKE.  I want to talk to you.

KENNY.  Sure.

DEKE.  Your father's giving a press conference out on the front lawn. He keeps telling everyone how you're innocent.

KENNY.    I know.

DEKE.    Have you ever talked to him about any of this?

KENNY.    No.

DEKE.    Kenny, do you understand exactly what went on to-day?

KENNY.    There's not gonna be any trial. Right?

DEKE.    Do you know why?

KENNY.    'Cause of my rights.

DEKE.    Do you understand all of this?

KENNY.    Yeah. I guess.

DEKE.    Kenny, do you realize what you did? *(Kenny does not respond.)* Talk to me.

KENNY.    You mean about Chrissy?

DEKE.    Yes. What you told me about.

KENNY.    I know I did it. It just seems ... like somebody else did it and I was just there watching. Like it was a movie or something. That's the truth Mr. Winters. *(Looks to Deke for reaction; none comes.)* You believe me about that, don't you Mr. Winters?

DEKE.    Yes.

KENNY.    I could tell you believe me. That day you yelled at my dad ... that wasn't really you. I watched you. I look like that sometimes ... *(He hands Deke the green notebook.)*

DEKE.    What's this?

KENNY.    Stuff I write. I want you to have it. *(Deke throws the notebook on the floor.)*

DEKE.    You killed a girl Kenny.

KENNY.    I know.

DEKE.    And you're not being punished for it! You should be but you're not!

KENNY.    I guess ...

DEKE.    There's no "guess" at all! You're sick — you need help or you'll do this again!

KENNY.    Maybe. I don't know ... *(Deke throws his lit cigarette at Kenny and grabs him by the shirt.)*

DEKE.    Don't tell me you don't know! You do!

MRS. SIMMONDS.    Mr. Winters! *(She attempts to break it up. Deke releases him.)*

63

DEKE. Your son got a lucky break Mrs. Simmonds. If you're smart you'll get him out of this town. *(He begins to cross away.)*
KENNY. Mr. Winters ... *(He stops. Kenny picks up the notebook, handing it to Deke.)* It's not that good or anything, just some stuff I wrote. I know you won't show it to anybody — confidential, right? — like you said that day in my room. Anyway I want you to have it. *(Deke takes the book.)* I'm not mad at you or anything. *(Deke moves away as O'Brien appears.)*
O'BRIEN. Mr. Winters?
KENNY. I understand ... *(Kenny fades.)*
O'BRIEN. Now that it's all over I want you to know that I bear no animosity towards you. You had a job to do — am I right? I don't even ... well, you may find this hard to believe but ... I can't ... bring myself to hate that boy anymore for ... what he did. Be sort of like hating a dog that bites you, am I right? And there's no sense in that, wouldn't you agree? *(Deke moves away as lights fade on O'Brien.)* You're a very capable man, Mr. Winters. Who knows, It's a small town. *(Carmella appears.)*
CARMELLA. Deke —
O'BRIEN. I may hire you myself someday. *(O'Brien dissappears as Carmella rushes to Deke.)*
CARMELLA. He's acting crazy. I don't know where he is.
DEKE. Where you movin' Carmella?
CARMELLA. He's supposed to be at a meeting. They called — he's not there —
DEKE. You got a sign on your front lawn. Where you movin'?
CARMELLA. *(Embarrassed.)* He doesn't want you to know. *(A beat.)* Find him.
DEKE. I'm the last person he wants to talk to —
CARMELLA. Find him! The man drove three hundred miles looking for you at least you can ... for God's sake do this for me, will ya Deke? I'm so scared ... *(She backs into the darkness. The sound of a train is heard and the lights find Vince — drunk — sitting alone. The sound of the train fades as Deke approaches. Vince holds a newspaper.)*
DEKE. You got your wife scared to death.

VINCE.   (Waving paper.) You read this? Hanh? You should hear somea the things they're sayin' 'bout me. Bet ya my old man don't buy thirty copies of this issue ... (He drunkenly throws the paper.) I think I'm gonna sue 'em. Be like everybody else ... sue their asses off. Know any good lawyers?

DEKE.   You're supposed to be at a meeting.

VINCE.   Fuck 'em. Let 'em hang me by the balls in abstentia. That the right word?

DEKE.   Carmella's worried.

VINCE.   You went to college — that the right word? (He begins to walk a tightrope on the rails.)

DEKE.   Come on Vince, get off the track.

VINCE.   I never beat you. Never won a gamea chicken. I'm about 0 for 400. That usta bug me. (He squats on the track.) We coulda got killed a million times playin' that. But you always stayed on longer'n ... always beat me. That one time it almost got parta your tennis shoe, 'member?

DEKE.   Yeah.

VINCE.   You'd look like you didn't give a shit whether that train squashed you or not.

DEKE.   (Quietly.) I didn't. (Silence.)

VINCE.   That kid's guilty Deke.

DEKE.   (Exhausted.) Vince ...

VINCE.   Just you and me here now. Our spot. He killed her, didn't he? (No response.) Didn't he?

DEKE.   You know.

VINCE.   You tell me.

DEKE.   C'mon, let's go home.

VINCE.   You tell me! (Deke says nothing.) He killed her. After he ripped her up with a pipe he killed her. But he don't go to jail cause I fucked up. Right? (Silence.) Right?

DEKE.   Right.

VINCE.   You wanta explain that to me.

DEKE.   I can't.

VINCE.   'Cause I don't get it, ya know. Maybe I'm just stupid, hanh? (Silence.) Basement fulla water ... bikes ta put together ... simple shit like that. But I'm inna big hurry and I didn't look hard enough ... and that girl was bein' crushed by wet cinderblocks while I was ten feet away from her. Maybe less ... I mean, ya know ... everything else ... losin' my job, bein' the town asshole ... I can move, right? Go someplace else, forget all 'bout it. But ... oh man, I wish I'd found her Deke. Maybe she even heard me but she couldn't make any sorta noise to let me know ... and she was in pain man. I've seen a few bodies ... they always look kind of relaxed — even accidents. Not her Deke. Her face was all scrunched up because he hurt her somethin' awful man ... he ripped her up and she felt it even after she was dead. And he'll do it again eventually ... I know that ... 'cause he's gotta demon.

DEKE.    *(Worried.)* Jesus Christ Vince ...

VINCE.    We'd make funna' my grandmother, 'member? She'd spit through her fingers and say somebody hadda' demon in 'em and we'd laugh at her. But after I become a cop I see she's not so crazy. There's people out there with demons in 'em, and this Simmonds kid ... *(He laughs.)* He's got some major league demons this kid has. And people like that gotta be locked up.

DEKE.    The system doesn't work that way Vince. It might be nice if it did but —

VINCE.    Then the system's fucked up —

DEKE.    What else we got Vince? Huh? Whatta ya wanta do — lock up everybody your grandmother spits at? Put away everybody who might be dangerous someday — that what you're sayin'?

VINCE.    Sounds good ta me —    *(A train is heard.)*

DEKE.    There'd be nobody left Vince —

VINCE.    C'mere ...

DEKE.    Knock it off —

VINCE.    C'mere ...

DEKE.    You're drunk. Get offa the track — it's not funny.

VINCE.    C'mere and get me off.

DEKE.    This is stupid. *(He crosses to Vince, grabbing him by the arm. Vince grabs him back, pulling him down. Train noise grows louder.)*

VINCE.    Come on ya pussy ... you won't get drunk with me, least play some chicken ... *(He links arms with Deke, who is still not cooperating.)* Gimme a chance to beat ya ... just once I wanta beatcha ... *(Directly into Deke's face.)* You owe me man ... *(Deke cooperates. They squat together, arms linked.)* All right! Brings back memories, hanh?

DEKE.   It was stupid then — it's stupid now.

VINCE.   You're gettin' old Deke. Where's your sense of adventure? *(Noise louder.)* Here she comes! *(Deke jumps to one side, rolling on the ground.)*

DEKE.   You win! Okay — you win! *(Vince does not move. The noise grows.)* Vince! *(Vince jumps to the same side, tumbling into Deke. The noise is deafening. They are entangled on the ground for a moment, Vince laughing.)*

VINCE.   Had ya scared didn't I? *(The noise begins to fade.)* Don't worry Deke. I'm not gonna kill myself. Specially like that. Know why? 'Cause the newspapers would all say somethin' like ... uhh ... "Dumb wop cop falls in fronta train ... " Somethin' like that.

DEKE.   *(Catching his breath.)* Jesus ... *(They sit up. Vince is still partially hanging on Deke.)*

VINCE.   You're my best friend man ... *(He kisses Deke, who is awkward.)* You never said it for me. Say it.

DEKE.   What?

VINCE.   I wanta hear you say it. I wanta hear it from you.

DEKE.   What Vince?

VINCE.   "He killed her." Say it. *(Deke says nothing.)* Say it!

DEKE.   He killed her. *(Deke takes his arm.)* Come on ... *(Vince yanks away violently.)*

VINCE.   Don't you fuckin' touch me! *(Vince begins to move away.)* Wanted ta hear ya say it.. I don't know why ... it's all over ... all over ... I just don't ... how could you do this to me? How? How ... *(He dissappears.)*

DEKE.   Where you moving to? Come on Vince — talk to me! Whatta ya say, huh? *(He moves to the couch, eventually lying back down as he did at the beginning of the play.)* Come on — please! Just ... talk to me ... please ... *(The voices heard at the beginning of the play start.)*

VINCE.   How could you do this to me? How?

CARMELLA.   I'm so scared ...

MR. O'BRIEN. Have any kids of your own Mr. Winters?
MRS. SIMMONDS. That's no way for any young lady to die ...
MR. SIMMONDS. That boy didn't kill anybody!
MRS. SIMMONDS. That's no way for any young lady to die ...
MR. O'BRIEN. Have any kids of your own Mr. Winters?
CARMELLA. I'm so scared ...
MR. O'BRIEN. Have any kids of your own Mr. Winter?
VINCE. How could you do this to me? How?
DEKE. Please! *(The voices stop abruptly as he bolts up. Diane says nothing as he looks at her. She wipes some sweat from his forehead. He rises unsteadily and finds the green notebook. He begins to tear it up, throwing pieces all over.)* I'll clean it up tommorrow. *(Diane nods. Deke sits on the couch and reaches for his tea cup. She stops him gently.)*
DIANE. Come to bed. *(Quietly.)* No ... *(She starts to take the cup away from him. He holds on.)* Far enough ... you slipped far enough. *(He stares at her a moment, unsure, then lets her take the cup. He curls his head into her lap.)*
DEKE. I'm freezin'.
DIANE. You did the right thing Deke ... it's all over ... shhh ... shhhh ... it's all over ... *(She strokes his head as the lights dim on them and rise on Kenny. Deke and Diane are still visible.)*
KENNY. Now that it's all over I thought I'd drop you a line to let you know everything is all right here. It's warm all the time and we get to go swimming a lot and my dad found a new job that he really likes and my new school is really nice. *(Lights begin to fade.)* Nobody here knows anything about what happened there and sometimes I think we ought to tell them but mom says no it's all over and let's keep it that way. I guess she's right. Anyway, that's all for now. Thanks for everything. I'll write again soon. Kenny. *(Lights fade on Kenny, then slowly on Deke and Diane.)*

# PROPERTY LIST

**Off-Stage Right**
New Year's noisemaker (DIANE)
New Year's party hat (DIANE)
New Year's streamers (DIANE)
Sandwich in plastic bag (MR. SIMMONDS)
2 Milky Way candy bars (MR. SIMMONDS)
Handcuffs (VINCE)
Police file with 2 black and white, 8 x 10 photos (DEKE)
Kenny's green notebook and pencil (KENNY)
Deke's green notebook (double of Kenny's) and pencil
    (DEKE)
Checkbook (DIANE)
Pen
Rubberband
Letter to editor (typed on sheet of paper) (O'BRIEN)
Brown purse (MRS. SIMMONDS)
TV remote control
Tie (Kenny)

**Off-Stage Left**
Tray (CARMELLA)
3 full beer bottles (CARMELLA)
1 unopened beer bottle (VINCE)
1 unopened can of Diet 7-UP (CARMELLA)
Newspaper with picture of Chief DelGatto on front page
    (VINCE)
Scissors
Dish towel
Tray with salami, knife, crackers (CARMELLA)
2 pieces of cake on plate
Extra plate
Cake knife

Purple towel (DIANE)
Brush (DIANE)
Mop (VINCE)
Broom
Drink (DIANE)

**On Stage**
Briefcase (DEKE) with:
    microcassette tape recorder
    legal pad
    small leather notebook
    silver pen and pencil
    miscellaneous files
Tissue (DIANE)
Ash tray with old cigarettes in it
Pack of cigarettes with 8 cigarettes (DEKE)
Tea cup with clear liquid
3 coffee mugs
Thermos of decaffeinated coffee

# COSTUME PLOT

## ACT ONE

**DEKE**

2-piece grey suit
Off-white shirt
Tie
Black belt
Grey socks
Black shoes

**DIANE**

**Voices - top of show**
Bathrobe
Slip

**Office — Deke meets Diane**
Lose:  Robe
        Slip
Add:   Slacks
        Cream blouse
        Blazer
        Gold earrings
        Necklace
        Watch
        Pantyhose
        Brown heeled shoes

**Office — "Mrs. Stein was here."**
Lose:  Slacks
        Blouse
        Blazer
Add:   Print dress
        Slip

**Diane's house**
Lose: Print dress
       Slip
       Pantyhose
       Necklace
Add: Teal top
       Leggings

**Office — "I can get that crazy bastard off."**
Lose: Leggings
       Teal top
Add: Pantyhose
       Slacks
       Print top
       Necklace

**VINCE**

**Voices — top of show**

Black cape and scarf
Police uniform: shirt, pants, tie, black shoes, black socks, holster and gun, black leather jacket, hat

**Welcome home Deke**
Lose: Black cape and scarf

**Coffee and cake at DelGatto's**
Lose: Police shirt
       Tie
       Holster and gun
       Jacket
       Hat
Add: Red T-shirt

**Christmas eve**
Lose:   Red T-shirt
Add:   Red plaid shirt with dickey

**Police station**
Lose:   Plaid shirt with dickey
Add:   Police uniform

**Hockey**
Lose:   Police shirt
        Jacket
        Hat
        Tie
        Holster and gun
Add:   Grey sweatshirt


## CARMELLA

**Voice — top of show**
Flowered blouse
Black pants
Black socks
Barrette
Black cape and scarf

**Welcome home Deke**
Lose:   Black cape and scarf

**Coffee and cake at the DelGatto's**
Same

**Christmas eve**
Lose:   Flowered blouse
Add:   Snowflake turtleneck
        Red knit jacket
        Earrings

**Hockey**

Lose:   Turtleneck
          Red knit jacket
          Earrings

Add:    Blue plaid shirt


**KENNY**

**Voices — "You do something really stupid."**
Corduroy slacks
High top tennis shoes
Grey socks
Belt
Short-sleeved black/green shirt

**Mr. Simmonds yells at Kenny**
Add:    Long-sleeved sweater

**"Her name is Karen."**
Same

**"I killed the fish."**
Same

**Police station with Vince and Mr. Simmonds**
Add:    Down jacket

**Kenny confesses**
Lose:   Down jacket
          Shirt
          Sweater
Add:    Grey sweatshirt

## MR. O'BRIEN

**Voices — top of show**
Navy blue blazer
Blue button-down shirt
Khaki-colored wool trousers
Brown socks
Brown leather oxfords
Striped tie
Eye glasses
Black cape and scarf

**"Chrissy's going to be cold..."**
Lose:    Black cape and scarf

## MR. SIMMONDS

**Voices — top of show**
Work pants
Work shirt
Belt
T-shirt
Heavy white socks
Boots
Cardigan
Black cape and scarf

**Mr. Simmonds yells at Kenny**
Lose:    Black cape and scarf

**Police station with Vince and Kenny**
Lose:    Cardigan
Add:     Grey work jacket
         Corduroy hat

## MRS. SIMMONDS

Voices — top of show
Slip
Plaid skirt
Pantyhose
White blouse
Cardigan
Flats
Black cape and scarf

**Mr. Simmonds yells at Kenny**
Lose:   Black cape and scarf

**Police station scene Vince and Kenny**
Lose:   Cardigan
Add:    Coat
          Purse
          Scarf

**Deke talks to Simmonds' at Police station**
Same

# ACT TWO

### DEKE
Same as Act One

### DIANE

**New Year's Eve**
Black dress
Black shoes
Coat
Black earrings
Coat

**Diane gives Deke a massage**
Lose:   Black dress
         Black shoes
         Pantyhose
         Black earrings
         Coat
Add:    Teal top
         Leggings

**Voices — end of show**
Lose:   Teal top
         Leggings
Add:    Bathrobe
         Slip


# VINCE

**Press conference**
Police uniform (without jacket)

**"When did you read him his rights, Vince?"**
Lose:   Police shirt
         Hat
         Tie
         Holster and gun
Add:    Brown sweater

**"Admit to me you were lying Vince."**
Lose:   Brown sweater
Add:    Green plaid shirt

**Vince admits to press**
Lose:   Green plaid shirt
Add:    Police uniform (without hat)

**Train tracks**
Lose:   Police shirt
          Jacket
          Tie
          Holster and gun
Add:    Grey sweatshirt
          Plaid jacket

**Voices — end of show**
Add:    Black cape and scarf

## CARMELLA

**"Admit to me you were lying Vince."**
Blue print top
Black pants
Black socks
Black shoes
Barrette

**"Find him Deke."**
Same

**Voices — end of show**
Add:    Black cape and scarf

## KENNY

**"My dad got me a TV."**
Corduroy slacks
High top tennis shoes
Grey socks
Belt
Striped knit shirt (worn over pants)

**"Mom"**
Same

**Deke at the Simmonds' pre-hearing**
Lose:   Corduroy slacks
           Knit top
           High top tennis shoes
Add:    Dress slacks
           Blue button-down shirt
           Jacket
           Tie
           Dress shoes

**"Do you know what you've done, Kenny?"**
Lose:   Jacket
           Tie
           Dress shoes
           Dress slacks
Add:    Grey sweatshirt
           Corduroy slacks
           High top tennis shoes

**Voices — end of show**
Lose:   Grey sweatshirt
           Blue shirt
Add:    Black/green shirt


**MR. O'BRIEN**

**Press conference**
Navy blue blazer
Blue button-down shirt
Khaki-colored wool trousers
Brown socks
Brown leather oxfords
Striped tie

Eye glasses
Black cape and scarf

**"My wife couldn't be at the hearing..."**
Same

**O'Brien and Simmonds press conferences**
Same

**"I bear no animosity..."**
Same

**Voices — end of show**
Add:    Black cape and scarf


## MR. SIMMONDS

**Deke at the Simmonds', pre-hearing**
Suit
Shirt
Tie
Light-weight brown socks
Raincoat (carried)

**O'Brien and Simmonds press conference**
Add:    Raincoat (worn)

**Voices — end of show**
Add:    Black cape and scarf


## MRS. SIMMONDS

**Deke at the Simmonds', pre-hearing**
Slip
Plaid skirt
Pantyhose
Chinese blouse

Flats
Earrings

**O'Brien and Simmonds press conference**
Add:    Coat
         Purse
         Pink sweater

**"Do you know what you've done, Kenny?"**
Lose:   Coat
         Purse

**Voices — end of show**
Add:    Black cape and scarf

# SOUND EFFECTS

Train sounds:   distant, approaching, loud and close, fading
Christmas music
Noisemaker (New Year's)
Party sounds (background)

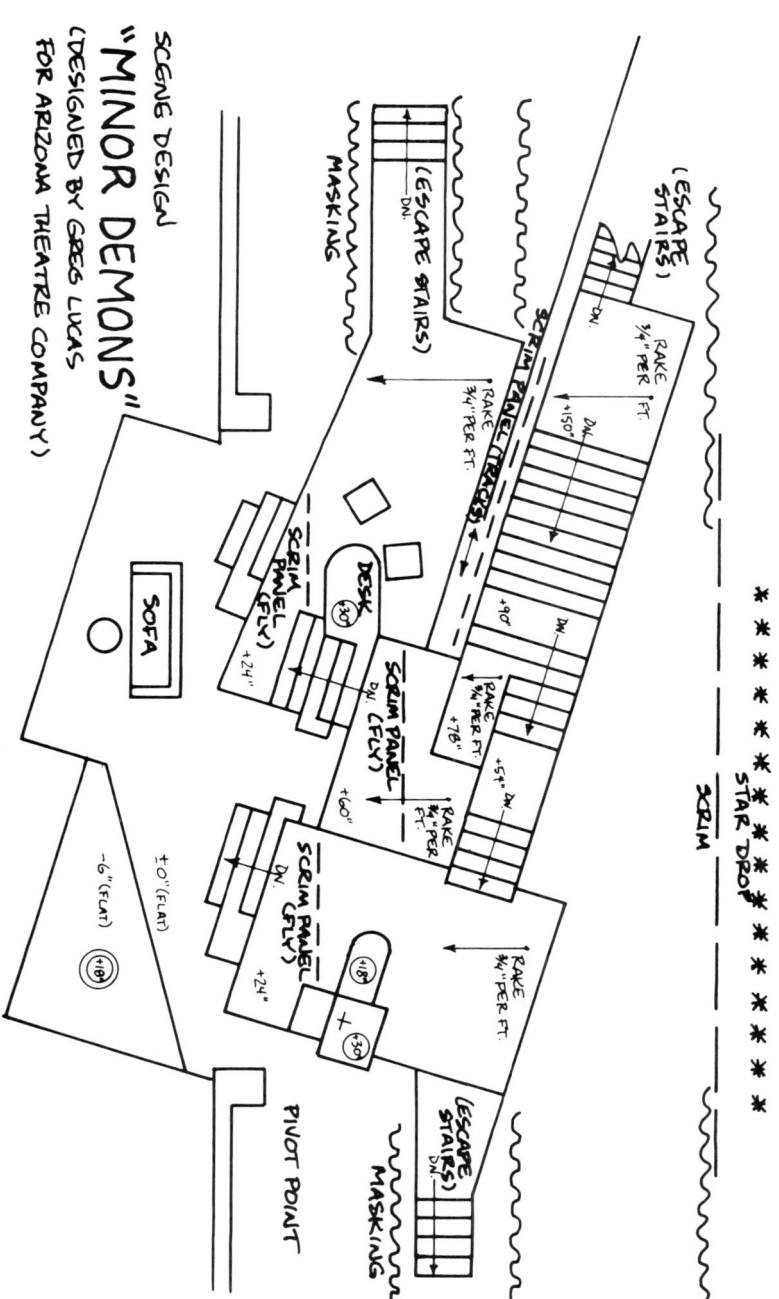

SCENE DESIGN
"MINOR DEMONS"
(DESIGNED BY GREG LUCAS
FOR ARIZONA THEATRE COMPANY)

# NEW PLAYS

★ **THE EXONERATED by Jessica Blank and Erik Jensen.** Six interwoven stories paint a picture of an American criminal justice system gone horribly wrong and six brave souls who persevered to survive it. "The #1 play of the year...intense and deeply affecting..." –*NY Times.* "Riveting. Simple, honest storytelling that demands reflection." –*A.P.* "Artful and moving...pays tribute to the resilience of human hearts and minds." – *Variety.* "Stark...riveting...cunningly orchestrated." –*The New Yorker.* "Hard-hitting, powerful, and socially relevant." –*Hollywood Reporter.* [7M, 3W] ISBN: 0-8222-1946-8

★ **STRING FEVER by Jacquelyn Reingold.** Lily juggles the big issues: turning forty, artificial insemination and the elusive scientific Theory of Everything in this Off-Broadway comedy hit. "Applies the elusive rules of string theory to the conundrums of one woman's love life. Think *Sex and the City* meets *Copenhagen*." –*NY Times.* "A funny offbeat and touching look at relationships...an appealing romantic comedy populated by oddball characters." –*NY Daily News.* "Where kooky, zany, and madcap meet...whimsically winsome." –*NY Magazine.* "STRING FEVER will have audience members happily stringing along." –*TheaterMania.com.* "Reingold's language is surprising, inventive, and unique." –*nytheatre.com.* "...[a] whimsical comic voice." –*Time Out.* [3M, 3W (doubling)] ISBN: 0-8222-1952-2

★ **DEBBIE DOES DALLAS adapted by Erica Schmidt, composed by Andrew Sherman, conceived by Susan L. Schwartz.** A modern morality tale told as a comic musical of tragic proportions as the classic film is brought to the stage. "A scream! A saucy, tongue-in-cheek romp." –*The New Yorker.* "Hilarious! DEBBIE manages to have it all: beauty, brains and a great sense of humor!" –*Time Out.* "Shamelessly silly, shrewdly self-aware and proud of being naughty. Great fun!" –*NY Times.* "Racy and raucous, a lighthearted, fast-paced thoroughly engaging and hilarious send-up." –*NY Daily News.* [3M, 5W] ISBN: 0-8222-1955-7

★ **THE MYSTERY PLAYS by Roberto Aguirre-Sacasa.** Two interrelated one acts, loosely based on the tradition of the medieval mystery plays. "... stylish, spine-tingling...Mr. Aguirre-Sacasa uses standard tricks of horror stories, borrowing liberally from masters like Kafka, Lovecraft, Hitchock...But his mastery of the genre is his own...irresistible." –*NY Times.* "Undaunted by the special-effects limitations of theatre, playwright and *Marvel* comic-book writer Roberto Aguirre-Sacasa maps out some creepy twilight zones in THE MYSTERY PLAYS, an engaging, related pair of one acts...The theatre may rarely deliver shocks equivalent to, say, *Dawn of the Dead*, but Aguirre-Sacasa's work is fine compensation." –*Time Out.* [4M, 2W] ISBN: 0-8222-2038-5

★ **THE JOURNALS OF MIHAIL SEBASTIAN by David Auburn.** This epic one-man play spans eight tumultuous years and opens a uniquely personal window on the Romanian Holocaust and the Second World War. "Powerful." –*NY Times.* "[THE JOURNALS OF MIHAIL SEBASTIAN] allows us to glimpse the idiosyncratic effects of that awful history on one intelligent, pragmatic, recognizably real man..." –*NY Newsday.* [3M, 5W] ISBN: 0-8222-2006-7

★ **LIVING OUT by Lisa Loomer.** The story of the complicated relationship between a Salvadoran nanny and the Anglo lawyer she works for. "A stellar new play. Searingly funny." –*The New Yorker.* "Both generous and merciless, equally enjoyable and disturbing." –*NY Newsday.* "A bitingly funny new comedy. The plight of working mothers is explored from two pointedly contrasting perspectives in this sympathetic, sensitive new play." –*Variety.* [2M, 6W] ISBN: 0-8222-1994-8

**DRAMATISTS PLAY SERVICE, INC.**
**440 Park Avenue South, New York, NY 10016  212-683-8960  Fax 212-213-1539**
**postmaster@dramatists.com  www.dramatists.com**

# NEW PLAYS

★ **MATCH by Stephen Belber.** Mike and Lisa Davis interview a dancer and choreographer about his life, but it is soon evident that their agenda will either ruin or inspire them—and definitely change their lives forever. "Prolific laughs and ear-to-ear smiles." —*NY Magazine.* "Uproariously funny, deeply moving, enthralling theater. Stephen Belber's MATCH has great beauty and tenderness, and abounds in wit." —*NY Daily News.* "Three and a half out of four stars." —*USA Today.* "A theatrical steeplechase that leads straight from outrageous bitchery to unadorned, heartfelt emotion." —*Wall Street Journal.* [2M, 1W] ISBN: 0-8222-2020-2

★ **HANK WILLIAMS: LOST HIGHWAY by Randal Myler and Mark Harelik.** The story of the beloved and volatile country-music legend Hank Williams, featuring twenty-five of his most unforgettable songs. "[LOST HIGHWAY has] the exhilarating feeling of Williams on stage in a particular place on a particular night...serves up classic country with the edges raw and the energy hot...By the end of the play, you've traveled on a profound emotional journey: LOST HIGHWAY transports its audience and communicates the inspiring message of the beauty and richness of Williams' songs...forceful, clear-eyed, moving, impressive." —*Rolling Stone.* "...honors a very particular musical talent with care and energy... smart, sweet, poignant." —*NY Times.* [7M, 3W] ISBN: 0-8222-1985-9

★ **THE STORY by Tracey Scott Wilson.** An ambitious black newspaper reporter goes against her editor to investigate a murder and finds the *best* story...but at what cost? "A singular new voice...deeply emotional, deeply intellectual, and deeply musical..." —*The New Yorker.* "...a conscientious and absorbing new drama..." —*NY Times.* "...a riveting, tough-minded drama about race, reporting and the truth..." —*A.P.* "... a stylish, attention-holding script that ends on a chilling note that will leave viewers with much to talk about." —*Curtain Up.* [2M, 7W (doubling, flexible casting)] ISBN: 0-8222-1998-0

★ **OUR LADY OF 121st STREET by Stephen Adly Guirgis.** The body of Sister Rose, beloved Harlem nun, has been stolen, reuniting a group of life-challenged childhood friends who square off as they wait for her return. "A scorching and dark new comedy... Mr. Guirgis has one of the finest imaginations for dialogue to come along in years." —*NY Times.* "Stephen Guirgis may be the best playwright in America under forty." —*NY Magazine.* [8M, 4W] ISBN: 0-8222-1965-4

★ **HOLLYWOOD ARMS by Carrie Hamilton and Carol Burnett.** The coming-of-age story of a dreamer who manages to escape her bleak life and follow her romantic ambitions to stardom. Based on Carol Burnett's bestselling autobiography, *One More Time.* "...pure theatre and pure entertainment..." —*Talkin' Broadway.* "...a warm, fuzzy evening of theatre." —*BrodwayBeat.com.* "...chuckles and smiles of recognition or surprise flow naturally...a remarkable slice of life." —*TheatreScene.net.* [5M, 5W, 1 girl] ISBN: 0-8222-1959-X

★ **INVENTING VAN GOGH by Steven Dietz.** A haunting and hallucinatory drama about the making of art, the obsession to create and the fine line that separates truth from myth. "Like a van Gogh painting, Dietz's story is a gorgeous example of excess—one that remakes reality with broad, well-chosen brush strokes. At evening's end, we're left with the author's resounding opinions on art and artifice, and provoked by his constant query into which is greater: van Gogh's art or his violent myth." —*Phoenix New Times.* "Dietz's writing is never simple. It is always brilliant. Shaded, compressed, direct, lucid—he frames his subject with a remarkable understanding of painting as a physical experience." —*Tucson Citizen.* [4M, 1W] ISBN: 0-8222-1954-9

**DRAMATISTS PLAY SERVICE, INC.**
440 Park Avenue South, New York, NY 10016  212-683-8960  Fax 212-213-1539
postmaster@dramatists.com  www.dramatists.com

# NEW PLAWS

★ **INTIMATE APPAREL by Lynn Nottage.** The moving and lyrical story of a turn-of-the-century black seamstress whose gifted hands and sewing machine are the tools she uses to fashion her dreams from the whole cloth of her life's experiences. "...Nottage's play has a delicacy and eloquence that seem absolutely right for the time she is depicting..." –*NY Daily News*. "...thoughtful, affecting...The play offers poignant commentary on an era when the cut and color of one's dress—and of course, skin—determined whom one could and could not marry, sleep with, even talk to in public." –*Variety*. [2M, 4W] ISBN: 0-8222-2009-1

★ **BROOKLYN BOY by Donald Margulies.** A witty and insightful look at what happens to a writer when his novel hits the bestseller list. "The characters are beautifully drawn, the dialogue sparkles..." –*nytheatre.com*. "Few playwrights have the mastery to smartly investigate so much through a laugh-out-loud comedy that combines the vintage subject matter of successful writer-returning-to-ethnic-roots with the familiar mid-life crisis." –*Show Business Weekly*. [4M, 3W] ISBN: 0-8222-2074-1

★ **CROWNS by Regina Taylor.** Hats become a springboard for an exploration of black history and identity in this celebratory musical play. "Taylor pulls off a Hat Trick: She scores thrice, turning CROWNS into an artful amalgamation of oral history, fashion show, and musical theater..." –*TheatreMania.com*. "...wholly theatrical...Ms. Taylor has created a show that seems to arise out of spontaneous combustion, as if a bevy of department-store customers simultaneously decided to stage a revival meeting in the changing room." –*NY Times*. [1M, 6W (2 musicians)] ISBN: 0-8222-1963-8

★ **EXITS AND ENTRANCES by Athol Fugard.** The story of a relationship between a young playwright on the threshold of his career and an aging actor who has reached the end of his. "[Fugard] can say more with a single line than most playwrights convey in an entire script...Paraphrasing the title, it's safe to say this drama, making its memorable entrance into our consciousness, is unlikely to exit as long as a theater exists for exceptional work." –*Variety*. "A thought-provoking, elegant and engrossing new play..." –*Hollywood Reporter*. [2M] ISBN: 0-8222-2041-5

★ **BUG by Tracy Letts.** A thriller featuring a pair of star-crossed lovers in an Oklahoma City motel facing a bug invasion, paranoia, conspiracy theories and twisted psychological motives. "...obscenely exciting...top-flight craftsmanship. Buckle up and brace yourself..." –*NY Times*. "...[a] thoroughly outrageous and thoroughly entertaining play...the possibility of enemies, real and imagined, to squash has never been more theatrical." –*A.P.* [3M, 2W] ISBN: 0-8222-2016-4

★ **THOM PAIN (BASED ON NOTHING) by Will Eno.** An ordinary man muses on childhood, yearning, disappointment and loss, as he draws the audience into his last-ditch plea for empathy and enlightenment. "It's one of those treasured nights in the theater—treasured nights anywhere, for that matter—that can leave you both breathless with exhilaration and...in a puddle of tears." –*NY Times*. "Eno's words...are familiar, but proffered in a way that is constantly contradictory to our expectations. Beckett is certainly among his literary ancestors." –*nytheatre.com*. [1M] ISBN: 0-8222-2076-8

★ **THE LONG CHRISTMAS RIDE HOME by Paula Vogel.** Past, present and future collide on a snowy Christmas Eve for a troubled family of five. "...[a] lovely and hauntingly original family drama...a work that breathes so much life into the theater." –*Time Out*. "...[a] delicate visual feast..." –*NY Times*. "...brutal and lovely...the overall effect is magical." –*NY Newsday*. [3M, 3W] ISBN: 0-8222-2003-2

**DRAMATISTS PLAY SERVICE, INC.**
**440 Park Avenue South, New York, NY 10016 212-683-8960 Fax 212-213-1539**
**postmaster@dramatists.com   www.dramatists.com**